TEACHER'S MANUAL

Evolution:
The Grand Experiment
Volume 3

Untold Stories of Human Evolution

by Dr. Carl Werner

Audio Visual Consultants Inc.
St. Louis, MO

ISBN: 9798876545367

© Copyright 2024, Audio Visual Consultants, Inc.

Copy Editor: Carla Azzara

First Edition: 2024 (Electronic book, first edition, Version 3)

Copyright © 2024 by Carl Werner. All rights reserved. No part of this book may be used or reproduced in any manner whatsoever without written permission of the publisher except in the case of brief quotations in articles and reviews. For more information contact the author through The Grand Experiment website listed below.

Please visit our website for other great courses:
www.TheGrandExperiment.com

Acknowledgments

I would like to thank my lovely wife Debbie Werner and Nick Wilson, whose invaluable help has made this all possible.

This one-semester class, entitled Anthropology 1, is designed for students 9th grade to adult (including college). It address the known problems with ape-men fossils. Teaching this class requires the accompanying textbook entitled, "*Evolution: The Grand Experiment Volume 3, Untold Stories of Human Evolution*" by Dr. Carl Werner. This textbook can be purchased through the Grand Experiment website (TheGrandExperiment.com).

There are two associated videos cited in this teacher's manual. They are not required but are incredibly helpful for the student and teacher, namely:

Episode 3, "*Untold Stories of Human Evolution*"

Episode 5 "*Human Evolution Fraud in North and South America.*"

These two videos are also available for purchase or rental through the Grand Experiment website. (The DVD shown below has both Episode 3 and Episode 5.)

PLEASE NOTE: An optional, highly-recommended, follow-up class, entitled Anthropology 2, is suggested for all. This second class coincides with the follow-up textbook, entitled "*Evolution: The Grand Experiment Volume 4, Nine Categories of Overturned Ape-Men.*"

SEE WHAT STUDENTS ARE SAYING:

Dr. Werner,

I'm now completely finished with the course! Here's my general review: The course has taught me a ton about human evolution and ape-men. Even though I've grown up being taught that evolution is false and even watched videos of yours on this topic before, I'll definitely look at supposed ape-men much differently after reading this book. <u>This book was so much more interesting to me and nicer to read (not boring) than any other schoolbook I can recall.</u> I think students will enjoy taking it, either as a class or just on their own like I did. I'd be happy to answer any questions. My final grade was 97%.

Hi Dr. Werner,
I finished chapter 2. I liked the chapter and how it was in a story format; easy to remember that way.

Dr. Werner,
I've watched the video section and thought it was good as a shorter version of the printed chapter containing the most important things to know, since it's difficult to remember everything from a long chapter.

Hi Dr. Werner,
Here are my notes for chapter 3 of the course. This was my favorite chapter so far, wanting to know how everything was gonna turn out (mainly between Dr. Osborn and Bryan) kept me turning the pages.

Hi Dr. Werner,
Done with chapter 5. Sorry this one took longer, I took spring break last week. I thought this chapter was very good. It was interesting seeing how many books supported the idea of the Orce Ape-Man even with the evidence clearing showing it not to be one.

Hi Dr. Werner,
I've finished chapter 6 of your course.
When I finished reading chapter 6 I was very surprised to find that the next chapter's name was "Conclusions." Somehow I had the idea that there were 10 chapters. Now I see there are really only 5 if you don't count the introduction and conclusion, that seems like the right amount to me. I haven't read the final chapter yet, so I'm interested to see what the <u>surprise ending</u> is going to be.

Nick

Final Class Grade Tabulation

Student Quiz	# Questions	# Correct Answers	Score %
Chapter 1 Introduction	10	_____	_____%
Chapter 2 *Tetraprothomo*	10	_____	_____%
Chapter 3 Nebraska Ape-Man	10	_____	_____%
Chapter 4 (1st half) *Prometheus*	10	_____	_____%
Chapter 4 (2nd half) *Prometheus*	10	_____	_____%
Chapter 5 The Orce Ape-Man	10	_____	_____%
Chapter 6 Libyan Ape-Man	10	_____	_____%
Chapter 7 Conclusions	10	_____	_____%
Comprehensive Final Exam	20	_____	_____%
Totals:	100	_____	_____%

Final Grade Based on Totals:
- 90-100% A
- 80-90% B
- 70-80% C
- 60-70% D
- <60% F

Teacher's Notes for Week 1
Teacher time for this class: 30 minutes

Step 1: The teacher reads the next five paragraphs out loud to the students to introduce them to the first lesson.

Human evolution is the theory that humans evolved from apes over millions of years. You may hear about human evolution on the internet, in books, in documentaries, or in science museum displays.

The purpose of this course, is to help you learn to differentiate between **facts** offered by scientists about human evolution and **opinions**. Many times, cold, hard, "**facts**" about human evolution turn out to be not true. Even worse, typically these "**facts**" are overturned years, decades and sometimes more than a century later. When facts are overturned, it becomes apparent that what was promoted as a "**fact**" by a scientist in his authoritative position was, in reality, just the scientist's *opinion*. Typically, when scientists presents "**facts**" to the public about human evolution or ape-men fossils or rock layers, they do not tell their audience that other scientists who believe in human evolution do not agree with their facts.

One example is shown on page 3 of your book. Turn now to page 3 in your book *Untold Stories of Human Evolution*. This beautiful, nearly complete, fossilized skeleton called *Oreopithecus* was discovered in Italy in 1958. Now look at the human evolution diagram at the bottom of page 3. *Oreopithecus* is the second animal from the left. For years, it was a scientific *"fact"* that *Oreopithecus* was an ape-man, a missing link in the evolutionary change from an ape to a man. It was portrayed as a direct human ancestor that walked upright like humans, not on all fours like apes.

Oreopithecus appeared in science journals, *The New York Times*, *Life* magazine and *Time* magazine. These stories about this full skeleton of *Oreopithecus* the ape-man were so compelling that some church leaders, including the Pope, began to accept that evolution was true. But, all of this information was wrong. Years later, *Oreopithecus* was shown to be just an **ordinary ape**. It was not an ape-man, it was not a human ancestor, it was not a missing link, and it did not walk upright like a human. Since then, evolution scientists have removed *Oreopithecus* from their theoretical evolution charts. In fact, all of the ape-men in the human evolution diagram on the bottom of page 3 have been shown to be false. In this chart, scientists now realize that the first three animals are ordinary apes and the last two are ordinary humans. The takeaway point of this story is this: (READ WITH EMPHASIS) It is a **fact** that "**facts**" given by experts are not really **facts** but ***opinions***. In most cases, these "**facts**" are overturned by other scientists, *years* later. You should not be as gullible as the rest of the public, believing everything you are told by a scientist.

Step 2 Class Discussion: The teacher now reads the Class Discussion Questions out loud. After the students try to give an answer, the teacher should help them get to the correct answer if needed. Encourage everyone to participate.

Class Discussion Question #1. Is it true that all scientists believe that humans evolved from apes? (Students should try to answer on their own.)

Answer (READ OUT LOUD): Some highly-qualified scientists (with PhD's in anthropology, geology, paleontology, genetics, chemistry, organic chemistry, cell biology, anatomy, biochemistry, astronomy, or physics) believe that humans evolved from apes over millions of years, but other highly-qualified scientists (with PhD's in anthropology, geology, paleontology, genetics, chemistry, organic chemistry, cell biology, anatomy, biochemistry, astronomy, or physics) do not believe in human evolution.

Class Discussion Question #2. What are the two theories how humans got here? (Students should try to answer on their own.)

Answer: (1) Evolution: Humans evolved from apes over millions of years.
 (2) Creation: Humans were created by a higher power or deity or God in a single, one time, event.

Class Discussion Question #3. Which theory of human origins (evolution or creation) do ape-men belong? Explain your answer.

Answer: Evolution teaches that apes evolved into humans over millions of years. According to this theory, the theoretical animals which were evolving from an ape into a human, are called ape-men.

Class Discussion Question #4. If humans were created suddenly by God and did not evolve from apes, would you expect to find ape-men fossils? Why or why not?

Answer: If humans were created and did not evolve from apes, there would be no such thing as an ape-men. Ape-men are theoretical animals, part of the theory of human evolution.

Class Discussion Question #5. If a scientist reports that he has found an ape-man, should you necessarily believe the facts that he or she reports in newspapers and science journals? Why or why not?

Answer: No. You should **not** believe a scientist's facts about human evolution. Most often, when scientists report that they found fossils of an ape-men, they do not tell you that other scientists, do NOT think the fossils are an ape-man and do not agree with his or her "facts."

Step 3: Students are told to read Chapter 1 now in class (only 3 pages long).

Step 4: END OF CLASS. Tell students there is no work until next class.

Teacher's Notes for Week 2
Teacher time for this class: 8 minutes

Step 1: The teacher reads this <u>out loud</u> at the beginning of class:

This is how this course works. Each week you will be reading a chapter from the book and then later you fill out the **Student Objective Sheet** for that chapter. (You should not fill out the **Student Objective Sheet** until after you read the chapter.) Then, you will be tested on the **Student Objective Sheet** for that chapter twice. First there is a quiz each week on the **Student Objective Sheet** that you filled out. Then at the end of the semester you will take a Comprehensive Final Exam on *all* of the chapters and all of the **Student Objective Sheets** you filled out during the semester.

THIS IS IMPORTANT: *You should carefully hold on to the **Student Objective Sheets** till the end of the semester as you will need them to study for the final exam. If you lose them you will have to start all over to study for the comprehensive final. Get a 3-ring binder and save your completed **Student Objective Sheets** to have them ready at the end of the semester to study for the Comprehensive Final Exam.*

ALL of the quiz and all of the final exam questions come off of the **Student Objective Sheets**. So if you carefully fill out the Student Objective Sheets, and study them for the quizzes and the final exam you should be able to score 100 percent on every exam and master the material quickly.

The reason there is a comprehensive final exam is I want you to retain this material long term, not just memorize the sheets to pass a quiz.

During the rest of the class today, you are to fill out the Student Objective Sheet for Chapter 1. Next week, at the beginning of class, you will take the quiz on Chapter 1.

Step 2: TEACHER: HAND OUT STUDENT OBJECTIVE SHEET FOR CHAPTER 1 (next page) and have the students fill them out now in class.

Step 3: End of class: Your homework is to study the Student Objective Sheet for your first quiz at the beginning of class next week. <u>Come prepared and see if you can get a score of 100%</u>.

End of Class Week 2

CHAPTER 1

Student Objectives Sheet for Chapter 1

By studying these objectives and knowing this core information, you should be able to pass the quiz next week.

1. The student should be able to name the natural history museum and city in which it is located where the top evolution scientist/Director (Dr. Henry Fairfield Osborn) concluded that humans did NOT evolve from apes (page 2). _____
_____

2. The student should know how many different species of ape-men were falsely created by a professor of anthropology at a national university (Dr. Florentino Ameghino) using bones dug up from the graves of recently buried human beings (page 2). _____

3. The student should know if the latest fossil ape-men discoveries offered as evidence offered for human evolution (*Homo naledi, Sahelanthropus tchadensis, Australopithecus sediba*) **are** or **are not** controversial among scientists who believe in human evolution (page 2). _____

4. The student should know how the scientific interpretation of the fossil *Oreopithecus* changed over time (page 3).
What was the *initial* interpretation of *Oreopithecus?* _____
What do scientists think of this animal today? _____

5. The student should be able to name the species names of all five animals in the human evolution chart on page 3, from left to right (for example, *Homo sapiens* or *Oreopithecus*).
Animal 1_____
Animal 2_____
Animal 3_____
Animal 4_____
Animal 5_____

6. The student should know what type of animal, each of the five animals in the human evolution chart on page 3 turned out to be (an ordinary ape, an ape-man, or a human).
Animal 1_____
Animal 2_____
Animal 3_____
Animal 4_____
Animal 5_____

Remember to study these answers for Chapter 1 quiz at the beginning of the next class! Come prepared to get a 100%

(END of Student Objective Sheet for Chapter 1)

This is the back side of a student handout page.

Teacher's Notes for Week 3
Teacher time for this class: 60 minutes

TEACHER STEP 1: Pass out the Chapter 1 Quiz which are on the next pages. (You can choose any one of the three sample quizzes provided, either Quiz A, B, C.) The quiz is only 10 questions long. **Grade the quiz** with the provided answer sheet (Either A, B, or C) and **record the students grade on page 3**.

AFTER QUIZ:

TEACHER STEP 2 READ OUT LOUD: The purpose of Chapter 2 is to show that even the top scientists can make mistakes when they identify fossils as being from an ape-man.

TEACHER STEP 3: Now the teacher leads the Class Discussion:

Class Discussion Question #1. Do you think it is possible that a majority of scientists, including those who work at the top universities such as Harvard and Princeton, could be wrong about a scientific theory? Can you give an examples?

Answer: Let students discuss.
EXAMPLE #1: The majority of scientists once thought the earth was the center of our solar system and that the sun orbited around the earth. This was proved wrong by Copernicus and later Galileo. The earth orbits around the sun.

EXAMPLE #2: The majority of scientists once believed in Spontaneous Generation. They thought that mice came from dirty underwear and that maggots and flies came from within rotting meat. All of this was disproved centuries later by Dr. Francesco Redi and Dr. Louis Pasteur. (This was discussed in Volume 1 of this book series.)

EXAMPLE #2: (Optional) Darwin and other scientists thought if you lifted weights and developed big muscles your children would be born with large muscles. This was wrong because your body cells do not pass information to the egg cells to pass genetic information on to the next generation. This false theory, called the Law of Use and Disuse, was disproved by August Weisman. (This was discussed in Volume 1 of this book series.)

Class Discussion Question #2. Do you think it would be possible for a *high level* scientist at a high level museum to misidentify an ordinary animal bone as an ape-man fossil?

Answer: Yes. Scientists are human and can be completely wrong. This applies to ALL scientists, including the Directors of top museums or Professors at top universities.

Class Discussion Question #3. The most famous scientist in South America is Dr. Florentino Ameghino. He was the Director of the National Museum of Argentina in Buenos Aires, Argentina. His ape-man was found at Mount Hermoso, Argentina. Can someone show me on the map on page 4 of your book where Buenos Aires is in relation to Mount Hermoso?

Answer: Turn to the map on page 7 in your book for the answer. Buenos Aires is North of Mount Hermoso.

TEACHER STEP 4: The students should now watch the first three minutes of the DVD entitled "*Episode 3, Untold Stories of Human Evolution.*" Insert DVD into DVD player. Hit "**Play**" and watch for 3 minutes. Stop when the two musicians quit playing music at around the 3 minute mark. IF you have rented Episode 3 (365 day rental) from our video on demand site (https://thegrandexperiment.vhx.tv) simply watch the first three minutes of the video.

TEACHER STEP 5: Next the students should watch the DVD segment on this same DVD that coincides with Chapter 2, *Tetraprothomo*. Hit "**menu**" on DVD remote. Select "**Chapters**" on the first screen of the DVD menu. Next, hit the button next to "*Tetraprothomo*." This segment is about 15 minutes long and goes to the end of the DVD. Once the DVD reaches the end, turn off the DVD. **Don't let the student watch the whole DVD yet.**

TEACHER STEP 6: Give Homework Assignment: For homework, read Chapter 2 this week. It is about Dr. Florentino Ameghino and the ape-man he found in South America. Chapter 2 is 36 pages long. It should only take about an hour to read. As you read it, think about the evidence of an ape-man the scientist finds. Also think about what he says the discoveries mean, and what they actually turned out to be.

Next week in class you will fill out the Student Objectives Sheet in class. (DON'T LET STUDENTS FILL OUT SHEETS UNTIL THEY HAVE READ THE CHAPTER.)

End of Class Week 3

Name:_____   Date:_____

Quiz for Chapter 1 (Introduction)
Quiz A

1. How many different species of ape-men were falsely created by a professor of anthropology at a national university (Florentino Ameghino) using bones dug up from the graves of recently buried humans? _____

2. *True or False*: Today, scientists believe *Oreopithecus* is an ordinary ape. _____

3. *True or False*: The latest, most up to date fossil evidence offered for human evolution (*Homo naledi, Sahelanthropus tchadensis, Australopithecus sediba*) is not controversial among evolution scientists. _____

4. What famous museum (including city where it is located) did the top scientist say that humans did NOT evolve from apes? _____
    _____   CITY:_____

5. *True or False*: *Initially* scientists thought the fossil *Oreopithecus* was an ape-man. _____

6. The fourth creature in the chart below is portrayed to be a human ancestor. What kind of animal did this creature turn out to be? An ape? An ape-man? A Human? _____

7. The third animal in the chart below is portrayed to be an ape-man. What kind of animal did this creature turn out to be? An ape? An ape-man? A Human? _____

8. The second animal in the chart below is portrayed to be an ape-man. What kind of animal did this creature turn out to be? An ape? An ape-man? A Human? _____

9. How many animals in the human evolution chart shown below turned out to be just ordinary apes or just ordinary *Homo sapien*s? _____

10. Give the <u>species names</u> of the five animals in the human evolution chart below, left to right. (Must name all correctly and in order to get a correct answer.) 1)_____ _____ 2)_____ 3)_____ _____ 4)_____ 5)_ _____

13

This is the back side of a student handout page.

Name:_____   Date:_____

Quiz for Chapter 1 (Introduction)
Quiz B

1. What famous museum (including city where it is located) did the top scientist say that humans did NOT evolve from apes? _____ CITY: _____

2. *True or False*: Even the latest, most up to date fossil evidence offered for human evolution (*Homo naledi, Sahelanthropus tchadensis, Australopithecus sediba*) is controversial among evolution scientists. _____

3. *True or False*: Today, scientists believe *Oreopithecus* is an ape-man. _____

4. *True or False*: *Initially* scientists thought the fossil *Oreopithecus* was an ape-man. _____

5. How many different species of ape-men were falsely created by a professor of anthropology at a national university (Florentino Ameghino) using bones dug up from the graves of recently buried humans? _____

6. The third animal in the chart below is portrayed to be an ape-man. What kind of animal did this creature turn out to be? An ape? An ape-man? A Human? _____

7. The second animal in the chart below is portrayed to be an ape-man. What kind of animal did this creature turn out to be? An ape? An ape-man? A Human? _____

8. What is the species name of the first animal portrayed to be an ape-man in the chart below? _____

9. How many animals in the human evolution chart shown below turned out to be just ordinary apes or just ordinary *Homo sapiens*? _____

10. Give the species names of the five animals in the human evolution chart below, left to right (Must name all correctly and in order to get a correct answer.) 1)_____ _____ 2)_____ 3)_____ _____ 4)_____ 5)__ _____

This is the back side of a student handout page.

Name:_____   Date:_____

Quiz for Chapter 1 (Introduction)
Quiz C

1. *True or False*: *Initially* scientists thought the fossil *Oreopithecus* was an ape-man.
_____

2. How many different species of ape-men were falsely created by a professor of anthropology at a national university (Florentino Ameghino) using bones dug up from the graves of recently buried humans _____

3. What famous museum (including city where it is located) did the top scientist say that humans did NOT evolve from apes? _____
_____ CITY:_____

4. *True or False*: Even the latest, most up to date fossil evidence offered for human evolution (*Homo naledi, Sahelanthropus tchadensis, Australopithecus sediba*) is controversial among evolution scientists. _____

5. *True or False*: Today, scientists believe *Oreopithecus* is an ordinary ape. _____

6. The fourth creature in the chart below is portrayed to be a human ancestor. What kind of animal did this creature turn out to be? An ape? An ape-man? A Human?
_____

7. The third animal in the chart below is portrayed to be an ape-man. What kind of animal did this creature turn out to be? An ape? An ape-man? A Human? _____

8. The second animal in the chart below is portrayed to be an ape-man. What kind of animal did this creature turn out to be? An ape? An ape-man? A Human? _____

9. How many animals in the human evolution chart shown below turned out to be just ordinary apes or just ordinary humans? _____

10. Give the <u>species names</u> of the five animals in the human evolution chart below, left to right (Must name all correctly and in order to get a correct answer.) 1)_____
_____ 2)_____ 3)_____
_____ 4)_____ 5)_
_____

17

This is the back side of a student handout page.

Answers for Chapter 1
Quiz A
Introduction

1. Five

2. True

3. False. It is controversial.

4. The American Museum of Natural History in New York City

5. True

6. A human (or *Homo sapiens*).

7. An ape

8. An ape

9. All (or five)

10. (Must name all correctly and in order to get a correct answer.) *Dryopithecus, Oreopithecus, Ramapithecus, Homo sapiens*, and *Homo sapiens*.

Answers for Chapter 1
Quiz B
Introduction

1. The American Museum of Natural History in New York City

2. True

3. False (Today scientists think *Oreopithecus* is an ordinary extinct ape.)

4. True

5. Five

6. An ape

7. An ape

8. *Dryopithecus*

9. All (or five)

10. (Must name all correctly and in order to get a correct answer.) *Dryopithecus, Oreopithecus, Ramapithecus, Homo sapiens*, and *Homo sapiens*.

ANSWER SHEETS

Answers for Chapter 1
Quiz C
Introduction

1. True

2. Five

3. The American Museum of Natural History in New York City

4. True

5. True

6. A human (Cro-Magnon Man or *Homo sapiens*)

7. An ape

8. An ape

9. All (or five)

10. (Must name all correctly and in order to get a correct answer.) *Dryopithecus, Oreopithecus, Ramapithecus, Homo sapiens,* and *Homo sapiens.*

Teacher's Notes for Week 4
Teacher time for this class: 15 minutes

TEACHER STEP 1: Before passing out the Student Objectives Sheet for Chapter 2, lead the Class Discussion about the Chapter 2. (The students just read this chapter for their last homework.) The following discussion should be informal and feel more like chit chat, rather than a formal deep discussion.

Class Discussion Question #1. Dr. Ameghino made many mistakes. In your opinion, what was the most outrageous mistake that Dr. Ameghino made? (Let each student answer this question.)

Answer: The students could select any number of his mistakes:
- Ameghino's ape-man leg bone which turned out to be from the raccoon family.
- Ameghino's ape-man neck bone which turned out to be from a recently buried human.
- Ameghino's ape-man "fireplaces" which turned out to be just lava rock (pumice).
- Ameghino's ape-man "baked clay" or pottery which turned out to be just rocks.
- Ameghino falsely claiming the neck bone was found in rock.

Class Discussion Question #2. Dr. Ameghino said all five of his ape-men were millions of years old. Was he right?

Answer: All five of Dr. Ameghino's ape-men had human bones taken from recently buried human graves so they were just hundreds of years old or less than that. (One of Ameghino's ape-men also had a leg bone from the raccoon family.)

Class Discussion Question #3. What was the highest degree Dr. Ameghino achieved in school?

Answer: He only graduated from grade school. He never graduated from high school. (His doctorate degree was just honorary.)

Class Discussion Question #4. Scientists have named a crater on the moon after Dr. Ameghino to honor his name. In Argentina, scientists named a museum library after Dr. Ameghino to honor his name. In Argentina, many schools are named after Dr. Ameghino to honor his name. In your opinion, do you think it is right that scientists still honor Dr. Ameghino as a great scientist?

Answer: Students give their opinion.

(Continued next page)

TEACHER STEP 2: Pass out the Student Objective Sheet for Chapter 2 (next pages). For the rest of class, the students should fill them out. Tell the students that if they don't finish the Student Objective Sheet for Chapter 2 in class, they have to finish as homework.

TEACHER STEP 3: READ OUT LOUD Prepare for the Chapter 2 quiz at the beginning of the class next week by studying and memorizing the Student Objective Sheet for Chapter 2. All the questions on the quiz come off of the Student Objective Sheets. Prepare and get a 100% on your quiz!

End of Class Week 4

CHAPTER 2

Student Objectives Sheet for Chapter 2 (3 pages)

By studying these objectives and knowing this core information, you should be able to pass the quiz at the beginning of class next week.

1. The student should know that Dr. Florentino Ameghino was considered *"one of the most eminent geologists and paleontologists of his day"* (page 5).

2. The student should know how many pages of technical writings Dr. Ameghino wrote in his lifetime (page 5). _____

3. The student should know what institution Dr. Ameghino <u>founded</u> at the National University of Cordoba, Argentina (page 5). _____
_____

4. The student should know the four types of ape-man cultural artifacts Dr. Ameghino found at Mount Hermoso (page 6). _____ _____
_____ _____

5. The student should know what "scoriae" is according to Dr. Ameghino (page 6, bottom). _____

6. The student should know what "tierra cocida" is according to Dr. Ameghino (page 6, bottom). _____

7. The student should know what large national newspaper reported Dr. Ameghino's discovery of ape-man artifacts at Mount Hermoso (pages 6). _____
What page in the newspaper did the article appear (pages 6)? _____

8. The student should know <u>what</u> ape-man <u>bone</u> was found at Mount Hermoso by Dr. Ameghino's brother Carlos (page 8). _____

9. The student should know what species name Dr. Ameghino assigned to the femur found at Mount Hermoso. The species name for the ape-man femur can be seen on the museum card in the top picture on page 8. (A species name consists of two Latin names such as *Homo sapiens* or *Canis familiaris*.) _____ _____

10. The student should know the definition of a habitual biped (page 9). _____
_____

11. The student should know the definition of a habitual quadruped (page 9). _____
_____

12. The student should know if apes are habitual quadrupeds or bipeds (page 9). _____

(Continued on next page)

23

CHAPTER 2

13. The student should know if humans are habitual quadrupeds or bipeds (page 9). _____

14. The student should know what form of locomotion (biped or quadruped) *Tetraprothomo* used according to Dr. Ameghino (page 9). _____

15. The student should know how many specific anatomical features Dr. Ameghino could see in the *Tetraprothomo* leg bone which demonstrated that *Tetraprothomo* walked upright like a human being (page 10). _____

16. The student should know what position (title) Dr. Ameghino held at the prestigious National Museum of Natural History in Buenos Aires (page 10). _____

17. The student should know who found the neck bone at Mount Hermoso and what Dr. Francisco Moreno and Santiago Pozzi thought about the *Tetraprothomo* neck bone. Did either think the neck bone was anything special? (Top of page 12) FOUND BY: _____ MORENO/POZZI OPINION: _____

18. The student should know what Dr. Ameghino initially though about the neck bone found at Mount Hermoso when he first saw it. Did he think it was anything special? (Bottom right of page 12) _____

19. The neck bone found at Mount Hermoso was the uppermost neck bone. The student should know <u>three</u> other names or abbreviations for the top neck bone of the body (page 13). _____ _____ _____

20. The student should know the names of the two types of stone tools Dr. Ameghino found along the coast of Argentina (page 16). _____, _____

21. The student should know how many species of ape-men that Dr. Ameghino eventually found in Argentina and be able to <u>write out their full species names from memory</u> (page 16). _____, _____, _____, _____, _____

22. Dr. Aleš Hrdlička came to investigate Dr. Ameghino's five new species of ape-men. The student should know what museum Dr. Aleš Hrdlička came from and what position did he held at that museum (page 19). _____, _____

23. The student should know Dr. Aleš Hrdlička found two witnesses in Argentina that indicated that Dr. Ameghino had lied about the neck bone of *Tetraprothomo argentinus*. What did Dr. Ameghino say about the neck bone and what did these two witnesses say about the neck bone that contradicted him (page 19).
AMEGHINO: _____
WITNESSES: _____

(Continued on next page)

CHAPTER 2

24. Dr. Aleš Hrdlička compared Dr. Ameghino's ape-man neck bone *Tetraprothomo argentinus* to the neck bones of modern apes and humans. The student should know what kind of animal Dr. Hrdlička concluded the neck bone was from <u>and</u> how old it was (page 20).
ANIMAL? _____
HOW OLD? _____

25. The student should know what <u>family</u> of animals the ape-man leg bone (femur) of *Tetraprothomo argentinus* belonged, according to Dr. Bordas (page 21).
FAMILY:_____

26. After looking at the pictures of procyonids on page 22, the student should know if procyonids are bipeds or quadrupeds. _____

27. The student should know if the leg bone *Tetraprothomo argentinus* was from a biped as Dr. Ameghino said or a quadruped. _____

28. The student should know what mammal <u>Order</u> raccoons (procyonids) belong (page 21)? NOTE, LEG BONE ORDER VS FAMILY. _____

29. The student should know what was ironic about Dr. Ameghino's mistaken identification of a procyonid leg bone as an ape-man (page 23). _____
_____

30. The student should know what Dr. Aleš Hrdlička concluded about the five ape men which appeared in Dr. Ameghino's human evolution charts on page 16 (answer on page 25).

31. The student should know what Dr. Ameghino's ape-man scoriae turned out to be (pages 6 and 26). _____

32. The student should know what Dr. Ameghino's ape-man tierra cocida turned out to be (pages 6 and 26). _____

33. The student should know the highest level of education Dr. Ameghino achieved (page 34). _____

34. The student should know what is the danger of assuming *that two bones found in close proximity to each other are from the same animal* (page 38 top left).
_____

35. The student should be able to name the six groups that promoted Dr. Ameghino as a hero after he died (page 40)? _____,
_____, _____, , _____,
_____, _____

(End Chapter 2 Student Objectives Sheet)

This is the back side of a student handout page.

Teacher's Notes for Week 5
Teacher time for this class: 40 minutes

TEACHER STEP 1: Pass out the Chapter 2 Quiz (*Tetraprothomo*) which are on the following pages. (You can choose from one of three sample quizzes, either Quiz A, B, C.) The quiz is only 10 questions long. Grade the quizzes with the provided answer sheet (Either A, B, or C) and record the grade on page 3.

TEACHER STEP 2: Read this <u>out loud</u> to the students: The purpose of Chapter 3 is to show that even the top evolution experts working at the top natural science museum in the world can misidentify ordinary fossils as ape-man fossils. Sometimes they also misidentify what body part the fossil bone is.

TEACHER STEP 3: Now lead the Class Discussion for Chapter 3 (Nebraska Man) with these questions:

Class Discussion Question #1. When you read a newspaper account, or an internet article, or see a television documentary about a scientist that has found a new ape-man should you necessarily believe it? Why or why not? (Students should try to answer on their own.)

Answer: Typically it takes decades, sometimes a century, to show that a reported ape-man was misidentified and is not an ape-man (examples being *Homo niger*, *Homo americanus*, Neanderthal Man which will be discussed in the next volume of this series). Sometimes these "ape-men" are human bones, monkey bones, ape bones, ordinary mammal bones (dog, cat, pig, etc.), and even reptile bones.

Class Discussion Question #2. Do you think it is possible that scientists at the top museum in the world (American Museum in New York City) would tell lies? Why or why not? (Students should try to answer on their own.)

Answer: If Dr. Ameghino told a lie about his *Tetraprothomo* neck bone being fossilized, it is possible that other top scientists could tell lies about their ape-man bones.

Class Discussion Question #3. Do you think it is possible that the top scientific experts at the top museum in the world, could identify a pig fossil as an ape-man? (Students should try to answer on their own.)

Answer: If you want the answer to this question, you will have to read Chapter 3 later in class to find out.

(Continued on next page)

Class Discussion Question #4. During the Scopes trial, which dealt with the issue of teaching the theory of evolution in public schools, newspapers and scientists portrayed Mr. William Jennings Bryan, who was defending creation, as a buffoon. Should you necessarily accept a characterization of someone by a third party if you have not met them? (Students should try to answer on their own.)

Answer: You should *never* accept another person's judgement about someone without further investigation. How would you like it if a newspaper characterized you as a bad person just because they disagreed with you on a point of politics or science or faith? Many times, people slander a person because they do not agree with their position on an issue.

Class Discussion Question #5. During the Apollo 13 Spacecraft mission to the moon, the crew radioed back to mission control in Houston base and said, *"Houston, We've Had a Problem."* What was the problem the Apollo astronauts had and why did these words become a common phrase in the English language?

Answer: The Apollo 13 spacecraft suddenly began losing oxygen and electrical power when it was 200,000 miles from Earth. The spacecraft appeared doomed to possible destruction including the loss of life of all those onboard. The astronaut's first words alerting mission control of this new dire situation, was a vast understatement. If would be similar to Dr. Hrdlicka wanting to notify his colleagues in Washington D.C. that all of the ape-men in South America included bones of recently buried humans and saying "Washington, We've Had a Problem." Or, it would be similar to a scientist notifying the American Museum in New York that their ape-man was a pig and saying, "New York, we had a problem." All three of these statements would be gross understatements describing a catastrophic situation.

TEACHER STEP 4: With the remaining time in class, the students should begin to read Chapter 3, entitled "*Hesperopithecus haroldcookii*, The Nebraska Ape-Man." This chapter is 47 pages long. It will take the students about 2 hours to read. DO NOT pass out the Student Objective Sheets until next week in class.

TEACHER STEP 5: Tell the students their homework is to finish reading the rest of Chapter 3 *Hesperopithecus haroldcookii*, The Nebraska Ape-Man. Dismiss Class.

(End of Teacher's Notes for week 4)

Name:_____   Date:_____

Chapter 2 Quiz (Ameghino's *Tetraprothomo*)
Quiz A

1. What species name did Dr. Ameghino assign to the leg bone found at Mount Hermoso? _____ _____

2–5. Name the four types of ape-man artifacts Dr. Ameghino found at Mount Hermoso.

_____

_____

_____

_____

6. What did Dr. Ameghino think the scoriae and/or tierra cocida found at Mount Hermoso represented? _____

7. What is another name for the uppermost neck bone? _____

8. Name the five species of ape-men that Dr. Ameghino eventually found in Argentina: _____, _____, _____, _____, _____

9. What was so ironic about Dr. Ameghino's mistaken identification of the ape-man leg bone found at Mount Hermoso? _____
_____

10. What did Dr. Ameghino's ape-man "scoriae" turn out to be_____

This is the back side of a student handout page.

Name:_____   Date:_____

Chapter 2 Quiz (Ameghino's *Tetraprothomo*)
Quiz B

True or False:

1. Humans and apes are habitual bipeds. _____

2. Dr. Ameghino thought the leg bone of Tetraprothomo was from a quadruped. _____

3. Dr. Ameghino had three earned PhDs in the sciences: Geology, Anthropology and Paleontology. _____

4. Dr. Florentino Ameghino was considered by his colleagues as one of the most eminent geologists and paleontologists of his day. _____

5. It is safe to assume that two bones found in close proximity to each other at a dig site are from the same animal. _____

6. Dr. Ameghino wrote more than 10,000 pages of technical writings in his lifetime. _____

Answer the following:

7. What did Dr. Aleš Hrdlička conclude about Dr. Ameghino's five ape men which appeared in his human evolution charts? _____

8. What mammal Order do raccoons belong? _____

9. What Family of animals (not ORDER) did the ape-man leg bone (femur) of *Tetraprothomo argentinus* belong? _____

10. What did Dr. Ameghino's ape-man "scoriae" fireplaces turned out to be? _____

This is the back side of a student handout page.

Name:_____   Date:_____

Chapter 2 Quiz (Ameghino's *Tetraprothomo*)
Quiz C

Match the following:

1. Leg bone of Tetraprothomo _____   a. False evidence of an ape-man fire

2. Neck bone of Tetraprothomo _____   b. Recently buried human remains

3. Pumice (lava rock) _____   c. Procyonid (raccoon family)

Answer the following:

4. What species name did Dr. Ameghino assign to the leg bone found at Mount Hermoso? _____ _____

5. Name the five species of ape-men that Dr. Ameghino found in Argentina:
_____, _____, _____,
_____, _____

6. What did Dr. Ameghino's ape-man fireplaces or "scoriae" turned out to be? _____

True or False:

7. The communist party and the socialist party promoted Dr. Ameghino as a great scientist and a national hero. _____

8. Dr. Aleš Hrdlička determined that all five species of ape-men that Dr. Ameghino found contained bones taken from the graves of recently buried humans. _____

9. Dr. Aleš Hrdlička found two witnesses in Argentina that said Dr. Ameghino lied about the neck bone of *Tetraprothomo argentinus*. _____

10. Dr. Ameghino could see 3 features in the raccoon leg bone which suggested it was from an upright walking, bipedal ape-man. _____

This is the back side of a student handout page.

Answers Quiz A
Chapter 2 Quiz (Ameghino's *Tetraprothomo*)

1. *Tetraprothomo (or Tetraprothomo argentinus)*

2–5. -stone tools

   -crudely carved bones

   -remnants of fireplaces (or scoriae or tierra cocida)

   -burnt bones

6. Fireplace

7. Any of these is correct answer: Atlas, or first cervical vertebra, or C1

8. *Tetraprothomo argentinus, Diprothomo platensis, Homo pampaeus, Homo sinemento,* and *Homo caputinclinatus*

9. Dr. Ameghino was a world expert in procyonids (raccoon family) yet he identified a procyonid leg bone as an upright walking ape-man.

10. Pumice or lava rocks

Answers Quiz B
Chapter 2 Quiz (Ameghino's *Tetraprothomo*)

1. False (Humans are habitual bipeds but apes are habitual quadrupeds.)

2. False (Ameghino believed the *Tetraprothomo* leg bone was from an upright walking biped.)

3. False (He only graduated from grade school and was a high school drop out. He never attended college.)

4. True

5. False

6. True

7. They all contained human bones from recently buried humans (less than 600 years old).

8. Carnivora

9. Procyonid

10. Pumice or lava rock

Answers Quiz C
Chapter 2 Quiz (Ameghino's *Tetraprothomo*)

1. C
2. B
3. A
4. *Tetraprothomo argentinus*
5. (Must answer all correctly to get credit.) *Tetraprothomo argentinus, Diprothomo platensis, Homo pampaeus, Homo sinemento*, and *Homo caputinclinatus*
6. Pumice or lava rocks
7. True
8. True
9. True
10. False (12 features, not 3)

Teacher's Notes for Week 6
Teacher time for this class: 5 minutes

TEACHER STEP 1: The students should now watch the first DVD segment covering the Nebraska Ape-Man. This segment is on Episode 5, entitled "*Human Evolution Fraud in North and South America.*" (Note, this is the first time the class has watched parts of this DVD.) Insert DVD into DVD player. Hit "**Chapters**" and select "**The American Museum New York**." Segment lasts about 7 minutes. Stop when the segment ends. IF you have rented Episode 5 (365 day rental) from our video on demand site (https://thegrandexperiment.vhx.tv) simply watch the first 12 and 1/2 minutes of the video. (Turn off when the University of Chicago segment begins.)

TEACHER STEP 2: Pass out the Student Objectives Sheet for Chapter 3 The Nebraska Ape Man (next several pages). Tell the students to work on this in class and if they do not finish they should complete on their own.

TEACHER STEP 3: Next week there will be a quiz on Chapter 3 so STUDY THE STUDENT OBJECTIVE SHEETS for the quiz next week.

This is the back side of a teacher page.

CHAPTER 3

Student Objectives Sheet for Chapter 3 (6 pages)

By studying these objectives and knowing this core information, you should be able to pass the quiz at the beginning of class next week.

1. The student should know Dr. Henry Fairfield Osborn was arguably the top evolution scientist in _____ _____ and Dr. Florentino Ameghino was the top evolution scientist in _____ _____ (page 42).

2. The student should know what museum Dr. Henry Fairfield Osborn was President of and for how many years (page 42).

3. The student should know what two Ivy League schools Dr. Henry Fairfield Osborn was a professor (page 42).

4. The student should know what science *organization* (not museum) Dr. Henry Fairfield Osborn was the President. *Time* magazine said, "*That presidency is the highest honor that U.S. and Canadian scientists can give a colleague*" (page 42).

5. The student should know who found the ape-man tooth in Nebraska (page 43).

6. The student should know the name of the dig site (quarry) and the state where the ape-man tooth was found (page 43).

7. The student should know the two *scientific* reasons the fossil ape-man tooth was of momentous importance (top of page 44).

8. The student should know who was leading the anti-evolution movement in the United States from 1904-1925 (page 44).

9. The student should know that William Jennings Bryan was not just an anti-evolution speaker but also a well known politician. The student should know what two different national political offices he held during his lifetime (page 46). (Not what office he ran for but offices he held.)

10. The student should know how William Jennings Bryan forced Dr. Henry Fairfield Osborn to respond publicly to his criticisms about human evolution (page 46).

11. The student should know that Dr. Henry Fairfield Osborn called Mr. Bryan derogatory names. What was one of the derogatory names he called Secretary of State Bryan (page 44)?

12. The student should know that Dr. Osborn formed a "Dream Team" of top scientists to analyze the ape-man tooth found in Nebraska. Three of the four scientists on the dream team specialized in what area of science (page 50 top).

(Continued on next page)

CHAPTER 3

13. The student should know what year and what setting Dr. Osborn announced the discovery of the ape-man tooth from Nebraska (page 52).

14. The student should know what species Dr. Osborn assigned to the ape-man tooth from Nebraska (page 52). _____ _____

15. The student should know that Dr. Osborn became obsessed with Dr. Bryan after their heated exchange in *The New York Times*. What derogatory term did he call Bryan during his speech before the Academy of Sciences (page 52).

16. Two scientists from the Natural History Museum of London disagreed with Dr. Osborn's interpretation that the Nebraska tooth was an ape-man tooth. The student should know what type of animal they thought Dr. Osborn's tooth belonged (page 54).

17. The student should know why Professor Grafton Elliott Smith thought "*One can, therefore, place implicit trust*" in Drs. Osborn's, Matthew's, and Gregory's claim that the tooth found in Nebraska was from an ape-man (page 56).

18. The student should know the title (be able to write out from memory) of the article that Professor Grafton Elliott Smith wrote for *The Illustrated London News* (page 57).

19. The student should know that *The Illustrated London News* printed a two full-page drawing (bottom of this page, below) of the Ape-Man of the Western World. The student should be able to recognize this drawing.

20. The student should know the 7-word (first) title of the article (be able to write out from memory) in *The New York Times* announcing discovery of the ape-man tooth in Nebraska (page 60).

21. The student should know how many anatomical features the Nebraska tooth had indicating it was from a chimpanzee-like ape-man with human features (page 62).

22. The student should know whether *The New York Times* did or did not make this statement about the ape-man tooth found in Nebraska: "In the whole history of anthropology no tooth has ever been subjected to such severe cross-examination as this now world-famous tooth of *Hesperopithecus*" (page 67). For extra credit during quiz be able to write this phrase out from memory.

23. The student should be able to write out <u>from memory</u> the four types of bone tools found near where the Nebraska ape-man was found: 1. skin dressers (for cleaning animal hides). 2. awls (used in sewing). 3. Necklaces (made of strung bones). 4. a tattooing comb (page 68).

(Continued on next page)

CHAPTER 3

24. The student should know how many bone tools were eventually found (total) at Snake Creek dig site (page 68).

25. The student should know that finding advanced bone tools at Snake Creek quarries substantiated what claim (page 68).

26. The student should know that Dr. Osborn said anti-evolutionist Bryan was ignorant, blind, dogmatic, deaf, a fanatic, a loud mouth, and a bigot (page 70).

27. Knowing now that the ape-man tooth turned out to be a pig tooth and the 3000 ape-man bone tools were just ordinary bones, what is your view of Dr. Osborn? Remember, Dr. Osborn described Bryan as ignorant, blind, dogmatic, deaf, a fanatic, a loud mouth, and a bigot. (Read all of Dr. Osborn's statements at the top and bottom of page 70 before answering.)

28. The student should know what statement Dr. Osborn made in his book *The Earth Speaks to Bryan* that was <u>revolutionary</u> (page 71).

29. The student should be able to write out *from memory* the three reasons why Dr. Osborn did not think humans evolved from apes (page 72).

_____

_____

_____

30. The student should be able to write out from memory the subtitle of the speech that Dr. Osborn gave at the American Philosophical Society (page 73).
1) "Let us _____

31. The student should explain why Osborn's speech was in conflict with his very own "Ape-Man of the Western World" and his 3,000 ape-man tools discovered from 1922-1927 (page 72).

32. The student should explain why this statement by Dr. Osborn is a lie: *"If you will examine carefully an exhibit in the Hall of the Age of Man* [at the American Museum below]*, you will see that it demonstrates very clearly **not** that man has descended from monkeys or from the apes, but that he has a long and independent line of ascent of his own"* (page 74).

33. The student should know what kind of animal the "Ape-Man of the Western World" turned out to be (page 76).

34. The student should be able to write out, from memory, the genus name of the extinct

(Continued on next page)

41

CHAPTER 3

pig that was identified as "*Hesperopithecus*, The Ape-Man of the Western World" (page 76). _____

35. The student should know that Osborn's ape-man tooth was not from the mammal order Primates but was from the mammal order _____ (page 76).

36. The student should know the other name for Artiodactyla (page 76). _____ _____ _____

37. The student should know that Dr. Osborn left out one **_critical_** piece of information when he gave his 1927 speech at the American Philosophical Society denouncing Darwin's ape-to-man theory. What **_critical_** detail did he leave out (page 76).

38. The student should know what two actions Dr. Osborn took to minimize the damage to his own career when the pig-tooth announcement was made to the press (top right page 76).

39. The student should know what animal *living today* looks similar to *Hesperopithecus*, the ape-man of the Western World (page 76 bottom). _____ _____ _____

40. The student should know that Dr. Osborn publicly derided former Secretary of State William Jennings Bryan for: 1) not believing that apes evolved into humans and 2) for not embracing the Nebraska ape-man fossil tooth (page 77). Write out why each of these criticisms made by Dr. Osborn is ironic?
1. _____
2. _____

41. The student should know the width of the headline (number of columns wide) announcing the discovery of the Nebraska ape-man (page 60), and the width of the headline retracting the story (page 78).

42. The student should know the original *The New York Times* headline announcing the discovery of the Nebraska ape-man used the words "*Ape-Man*" but the article retracting the story did not use the word ape-man in the headline, effectively minimizing the impact of announcing this science catastrophe by the American Museum (page 78).

43. The student should know that only after the Nebraska ape-man was determined to be a pig, all of the 3,000 bone tools were determined to be just ordinary animal bones. In other words, the "*skin dressers for cleaning animal hides, pointed awl-like implements evidently used in sewing, neck ornaments made of strung bones* [bones strung into a necklace], *and a kind of comb that seems to be a tattooing implement*" were just ordinary animal bones that had never been used as "tools" (page 80).

44. The student should know why the Nebraska ape-man might not be just a simple mistake but a fraud (page 81). IMPORTANT.

(Continued on next page)

42

CHAPTER 3

45. The student should know that although Dr. Osborn reported finding a tooth of an ape-man in 1922, he and his colleagues knew since 1909 that pig teeth at Snake Creek look like the molar teeth of humans and apes (page 81).

46. Besides withholding information that pig teeth found at Snake Creek quarry in Nebraska look like human teeth, the student should know some of the "audacious lies" that Dr. Osborn told (page 81 right middle and bottom).

47. The student should know what honor evolution scientists bestowed upon Dr. Osborn after it was revealed that he had misidentified a pig tooth as an ape-man (page 82).

48. The student should know if the Board of Directors at the American Museum did or did not punish Dr. Osborn for making the Nebraska blunder (page 82).

49. The student should know that Dr. Osborn predicted that the Nebraska ape-man had a flat face like a human, not a protuberant snout like an ape. In reality how protuberant was the face of *Hesperopithecus* (page 83 and page 79 bottom). Hint, look at the face of the animal this fossil turned out to be and decide if the lower part of the face (snout) sticks out or is flat like a human.

50. The student should know that the reliability of any fossil interpretation is proportional to what determination (page 84).

51. The student should know that scientists may withhold critical information about their ape-man fossil (page 84).

52. The student should know when a fossil "ape-man" is found at a dig site, it should always be compared to what type of animals (page 85).

53. The student should know that two-page drawing of the Nebraska Ape-Man which appeared in *The Illustrated London News* (below) should have depicted as what (based on the fossils) (page 85).

54. The student should view human evolution charts as what (page 86)?

55. The student should know scientists frequently justify that their fossil is an ape-man because the fossil _____ (page 87).

56. The student should know *why* it is problematic for scientists to argue that their fossil is an ape-man because it was found in the *correct and expected rock layer* (page 87).

(Continued on next page)

CHAPTER 3

57. The student should know that Dr. Ameghino (Chapter 2) said his ape-man *Tetraprothomo argentinus* was _____ years old, but Dr. Hrdlička determined it was _____ years old (page 87).

58. The student should know the range of dates given by evolution scientists for the Nebraska Ape man tooth and dig site (page 88).

59. The student should know how many different age determinations were made of the Nebraska ape man (each determination is in blue, right column page 87).

(End Chapter 3 Student Objectives)

Teacher's Notes for Week 7
Teacher time for this class: 40 minutes

TEACHER STEP 1: Pass out the Chapter 3 Quiz (Nebraska Ape-Man *Hesperopithecus*) which are on the following pages. (You can choose from one of three sample quizzes, either Quiz A, B, C.) The quiz is only 10 questions long. Grade the quiz with the provided answer sheet (Either A, B, or C) and record the grade.

AFTER QUIZ

TEACHER STEP 2: (Optional. This is redundant but students may need to hear it again.) Read this out loud to the students: The purpose of Chapter 4 is to show that even the top evolution experts working at the top natural science museum in the world can misidentify ordinary animals as an ape-man fossils. They sometimes have non only misidentified what animal the fossil came from but also what body part the fossil bone is.

TEACHER STEP 3: The students should now watch the first three minutes of the DVD entitled "*Episode 3, Untold Stories of Human Evolution.*" Hit "**Play**" and watch for 3 minutes. Stop when the two musicians quit playing music at around the 3 minute mark. IF you have rented Episode 3 (365 day rental) from our video on demand site (https://thegrandexperiment.vhx.tv) simply watch the first 3 minutes of the video. (Turn off when the musicians quit playing music.)

TEACHER STEP 4: Next watch the DVD segment on this same DVD that you just watched that coincides with Chapter 4, Prometheus. Hit "**menu**" on DVD remote. Select "**Chapters.**" Select "**Prometheus.**" This segment is about 20 minutes long. Once this segment is done, the typing on the screen with keyboard sounds starts for next segment, turn off the DVD. **Don't let the student watch the whole DVD yet.**

TEACHER STEP 5: With the remaining time in class, the students should begin to read the first half of Chapter 4, pages 89-121. Chapter 4 is entitled "*Australopithecus prometheus* (Ape Man of 2001: A Space Odyssey)."

TEACHER STEP 6: Tell the students to finish reading the first half of this chapter, pages 89-121 for their homework. Next week, in class you will receive the Student Objective Sheet.

Dismiss Class

This is the back side of a teacher page.

Name:_____   Date:_____

Chapter 3 Quiz (The Nebraska Ape-Man)
Quiz A

1. What museum was Dr. Henry Fairfield Osborn President?
_____

2. Two scientists from the Natural History Museum of London disagreed with Dr. Osborn's interpretation of the Nebraska ape-man tooth. What type of animal did they think Dr. Osborn's tooth belonged? _____

3. Write out from memory the subtitle of the speech that Dr. Osborn gave at the American Philosophical Society. "Let us _____

4. The reliability of any fossil interpretation is proportional to what determination?
_____

5. Write out the four types of "bone tools" found near where the Nebraska ape-man was discovered. _____, _____, _____, _____

6. What is the danger about critical information/evidence in human evolution? _____
_____

7. What *critical* piece of information did Dr. Osborn leave out in his 1927 speech at the American Philosophical Society when he denounced Darwin's ape-to-man theory? _____
_____

8. How many columns wide was the headline announcing the discovery of the Nebraska ape-man in *The New York Times*? _____

9. How many columns wide was the headline retracting the Nebraska ape-man in *The New York Times*? _____

10. What was so ironic about Dr. Osborn criticizing William Jennings Bryan for not agreeing that the fossil tooth found in Nebraska was an ape-man? _____
_____

For One Extra Credit Point

11. Write out the *The New York Times* statement which said the Nebraska ape-man tooth had been investigated thoroughly by evolution scientists. (Approximately 25 words.)

_____
_____
_____

47

This is the back side of a student handout page.

Name:_____   Date:_____

Chapter 3 Quiz (The Nebraska Ape-Man)
Quiz B

True or False:

1. During the course of his career, Dr. Osborn told several lies about ape-men. _____

2. Osborn's ape-man tooth was, in reality, from the mammal order Primates. _____

3. Before Dr. Osborn reported finding a tooth of an ape-man in 1922, he and his colleagues knew that pig teeth at Snake Creek look like the molar teeth of humans and apes. _____

4. Dr. Osborn publicly derided former Secretary of State William Jennings Bryan for: 1) not believing that apes evolved into humans and 2) for not embracing the Nebraska ape-man fossil tooth. _____

5. The Nebraska Ape-Man fiasco was likely a fraud, not just a simple mistake. _____

Answer the following:

6. When a fossil "ape-man" is found at a dig site, it should always be compared to what type of animals? _____

7. Who found the ape-man tooth in Nebraska? _____

8. What species did Dr. Osborn assign to the ape-man tooth from Nebraska?
_____   _____

9. How many anatomical features did the Nebraska tooth have indicating it was from a chimpanzee-like ape with human features (an ape-man tooth)? _____

10. Name one of the three reasons why Dr. Osborn did not think humans evolved from apes.
_____

For One Extra Credit Point

11. Write out the *The New York Times* statement which said the Nebraska ape-man tooth had been investigated thoroughly by evolution scientists. (Approximately 25 words.)

_____

_____

_____

This is the back side of a student handout page.

Name:_____   Date:_____

Chapter 3 Quiz (The Nebraska Ape-Man)
Quiz C

Answer the following:

1. Dr. Ameghino (Chapter 2) said his ape-man *Tetraprothomo argentinus* was _____ years old, but Dr. Hrdlička determined it was _____ years old.

2. Why it is problematic for scientists to argue that their fossil is an ape-man because it was found in the *correct and expected rock layer?*

3. What honor did evolution scientists bestow upon Dr. Osborn after it was revealed that he had misidentified a pig tooth as an ape-man? _____
_____

4. What was the name of the dig site (quarry) and the state where Dr. Osborn's ape-man tooth was found? _____

5. Dr. Osborn formed a "Dream Team" of scientists to analyze the ape-man tooth found in Nebraska. Three of the four scientists on the dream team specialized and had expertise in what area of science? _____

6. What animal *living today* looks similar to *Hesperopithecus*, the "Ape-Man of the Western World."? _____ _____ _____

7. The full two-page drawing which appeared in *The Illustrated London News* (right) of an ape-man standing in a field with a stone tool in his hand should have been depicted as what scene based on the fossils? _____

True or False:

8. Long before Dr. Osborn reported finding an ape-man tooth at Snake Creek, he and his colleagues knew that pig teeth at Snake Creek look like the molar teeth of humans and apes. _____

9. In reality the face of *Hesperopithecus* was flat like a human. _____

10. Different scientists determined the Nebraska ape-man to be 6 different ages. _____

For One Extra Credit Point

11. Write out the *The New York Times* statement which said the Nebraska ape-man tooth had been investigated thoroughly by evolution scientists. (Approximately 25 words.)

_____
_____
_____

51

This is the back side of a student handout page.

Answers Quiz A
Chapter 3 Quiz (The Nebraska Ape-Man)

1. The American Museum of Natural History or AMNH or American Museum
2. Bear
3. "Let Us Abandon the Ape-Human Theory"
4. The completeness of the skeleton
5.   -skin dressers (for cleaning animal hides).

    -awls (used in sewing)

    -necklaces (made of strung bones)

    -a tattooing comb
6. Critical evidence may be withheld by scientists
7. That the ape-man from Snake Creek was a pig tooth.
8. Four
9. One
10. Later Dr. Osborn would have to admit the tooth was not an ape-man but a pig.

EXTRA CREDIT.

11. "In the whole history of anthropology no tooth has ever been subjected to such severe cross-examination as this now world-famous tooth of *Hesperopithecus*."

Answers Quiz B
Chapter 3 Quiz (The Nebraska Ape-Man)

1. True
2. False (it was from the mammal order Artiodactyla or even-toed ungulates)
3. True (since 1909)
4. True
5. True
6. The other animals found at that same dig site
7. Harold Cook
8. *Hesperopithecus haroldcookii*
9. Eleven
10. Any one of these three answers:

    (a) the arm and leg bones of Neanderthal Man and Java Man were too human-looking to be considered ape-men,

    (b) Cro-Magnon Man's brain was larger than the average living European human, too big to be considered a missing link,

    (c) the similarities of apes and humans did not necessarily mean apes evolved into humans.

ANSWER SHEETS

53

Answers Quiz C
Chapter 3 Quiz (The Nebraska Ape-Man)

1. - more than five million years old,
   - less than 600 years old
2. It is *common* for other scientists to assign the same fossil to vastly different ages
3. President of the American Association for the Advancement of Science (or AAAS)
4. Snake Creek quarries, Nebraska
5. Fossil mammal teeth
6. The Eurasian wild pig (or *Sus scrofa*)
7. A pig
8. True
9. False (pigs snout stick out very far)
10. True

EXTRA CREDIT.

11. "In the whole history of anthropology no tooth has ever been subjected to such severe cross-examination as this now world-famous tooth of *Hesperopithecus*."

Teacher's Notes for Week 8
Teacher time for this class: 30 minutes

TEACHER STEP 1: Read this <u>out loud</u> to the students:

Last week in class you started to read Chapter 4, which is about Dr. Raymond Dart. He is considered one of the fathers of the theory of human evolution because he found the **first** australopithecine fossil (the Taung Child) and then found a second australopithecine, the supposed fire-using and tool-using ape-man named *Australopithecus prometheus*. This is the same ape-man which appeared in the movie *2001 a Space Odyssey*. The problem is that Dr. Dart **made up** many of the facts about his ape-men.

Dr. Dart's colleagues thought Dr. Dart was a big story teller, describing inconsequential fossils in melodramatic form as evidence he had found an ape-man. It took nearly **a half century to find out that most of the facts Dr. Dart presented were made up**.

TEACHER STEP 2: Pass out the **Student Objectives Sheet** "First Half of Chapter 4" (following pages). Because Chapter 4 is so long it has been broken up into two sections, the first half and the second half. Tell the students to work on Student Objectives now in class. There are more than 60 objectives to fill out. What they don't finish in class is your homework. THERE WON'T BE A QUIZ NEXT WEEK, BUT INSTEAD STUDY TIME TO PREPARE FOR THE NEXT QUIZ.

Dismiss Class

This is the back side of a teacher page.

CHAPTER 4 PART 1

Student Objectives Sheet for First Half of Chapter 4
Australopithecus prometheus (6 pages)

By studying these objectives and knowing this core information, you should be able to pass the quiz at the beginning of class next week.

The student should know that Dr. Dart basically found two ape-men. It is imperative that the student not get these confused. The first ape-man was The Taung Child (*Australopithecus africanus*) found in 1924. The second ape-man was the adult fire-using, bone-tool using Prometheus, (*Australopithecus prometheus*) found in 1947. The student should be able to recreate this chart below from memory. You will see that many of the student objectives can be answered from this chart:

	Dart's First Ape-Man	Dart's Second Ape-Man
Year:	1924/1925	1947
Common name:	Taung Child	Prometheus
Location:	Taung Quarry, South Africa	Makapansgat Cave, South Africa
Species name:	*Australopithecus africanus*	*Australopithecus prometheus*
Developmental age:	Child	Adult
Initial reaction:	Initially rejected by scientists	Initially accepted by scientists
Why this reaction?	Infant ape skulls look like humans	Found with fire residue / tools
Fossil:	Face/front skull/brain endocast	MLD 1 Skull fragment + others
Human Character 1	Flat vertical face	Human-shaped pelvis
Human Character 2	No eyebrow ridges	Human-shaped collarbone
Human Character 3	Forward positioned spinal cord	Human-sized brain, 1000 cc

1. The student should know where the tool using *Australopithecus prometheus* was found, (both the cave name and the country) (page 89).

2. The student should know what kind of doctor Dr. Dart was (page 90).

3. The student should know that Dr. Dart's colleague said this about Dr. Dart's first discovery the Taung Child: Dr. Dart "*made one of the greatest discoveries in the world's history*" (page 90).

4. The student should know that early on in his career, Dr. Dart was heavily influenced by the pro-evolution scientist Dr. Grafton Elliot Smith, an expert on brain anatomy. Dart was entranced by his brilliance and persona (page 90).

5. The student should know that even though Dr. Dart was entranced by the "brilliance and persona" of Dr. Grafton Elliot Smith, many of the ape-men promoted by Dr. Smith were later overturned. How many of the famous ape-men that Dr. Grafton Elliot Smith endorsed turned out to be not ape-men? The student should also write out their names from memory (page 91).

(Continued on next page)

CHAPTER 4 PART 1

6. The student should know <u>what kind of animal</u> the Piltdown Man, heavily endorsed by Dr. Grafton Elliot Smith, turned out to be (page 91).

7. The student should know <u>what kind of animal</u> the Nebraska ape-man, heavily endorsed heavily by Dr. Grafton Elliot Smith, turned out to be (page 91).

8. The student should know <u>what kind of animal</u> the Neanderthal ape-man, heavily endorsed heavily by Dr. Grafton Elliot Smith, turned out to be (page 91).

9. The student should know <u>what chairmanship</u> Dr. Dart held and at what institution (page 90).

10. The student should know what is the scientific name for a "mold of the inside of the skull (made of sediment)" (page 92).

11. The student should know which of Dr. Dart's two ape-men was composed of a skull and endocranial cast (page 92).

12. The student should know what was the <u>developmental</u> age of the Taung Child in human years (based on the presence of a permanent molar tooth in the jaw) (page 92).

13. Dr. Dart essentially found two important ape-men. The student should know the formal scientific species name for his first ape-man, the Taung Child (page 92), and the formal scientific species name for his second ape-man (page 102). (Species names are usually Latin and usually two names.)

14. The student should know <u>what year</u> the Taung Child skull (*Australopithecus africanus*) was found (top of page 92) and <u>what year his second ape-man skull fragment fossil was found</u> at Makapansgat (*Australopithecus prometheus*) (top page 102).

15. The student should know the vastly different reactions Dr. Dart received from his colleagues when he announced his two ape-men. What reaction did Dr. Dart receive after he published his interpretation of the Taung Child as an ape-man in the science journal *Nature* (page 92)? What reaction Dr. Dart received from his colleagues after he announced he had found evidence of a fire-using, tool-using, head bashing ape-man at Makapansgat (page 103)?

16. The student should know what kind of animal Dr. Dart thought the Taung Child was (page 92).

17. The student should know Dr. Dart thought the Taung Child was an ape-man because it had these three human traits: flat vertical face, absent eyebrow ridges, and central spinal cord opening (page 92).

18. The student should know that it is a the commonly known fact that *modern baby ape* skulls look similar to modern adult human skulls (page 92).

(Continued on next page)

CHAPTER 4 PART 1

19. The student should know that the forehead of adult chimpanzee skulls is what angle (pages 92-93).

20. The student should know that the forehead of adult human skulls is what angle (pages 92-93).

21. The student should know that the forehead of INFANT chimpanzee skulls is what angle (pages 92-93).

22. The student should know that the forehead of the infant Taung Child skull was nearly vertical similar to a modern adult human skull (pages 92-93).

23. The student should know that adult chimpanzee skulls have what size eyebrow ridges (pages 92-93).

24. The student should know that adult human skulls have what size eyebrow ridges (pages 92-93).

25. The student should know that INFANT chimpanzee skulls have what size eyebrow ridges (pages 92-93).

26. The student should know that the eyebrow ridges of the infant Taung Child skull are absent because it is an infant and this makes it look like an adult human (pages 92-93).

27. The student should know whether adult chimpanzee skulls have a protuberant face (muzzle) or a flat vertical face (pages 92-93).

28. The student should know whether adult human skulls have a protuberant face (muzzle) or a flat vertical face (pages 92-93).

29. The student should know whether INFANT chimpanzee skulls have a protuberant face (muzzle) or a flat face (pages 92-93).

30. The student should know that INFANT chimpanzee skulls and the infant Taung Child look like adult human skulls as far as the amount that the face sticks out (pages 92-93) and that this is not evidence of evolution but is evidence the Taung Child skull is an infant.

31. The student should know that adult chimpanzee skulls the spinal cord enters towards the back of the skull (pages 92-93).

32. The student should know in adult human skulls the spinal cord enters near the center of the bottom of the skull (pages 92-93).

33. The student should know in INFANT chimpanzee skulls and the infant Taung Child skull the spinal cord enters near the center of the bottom of the skull similar to an adult

(Continued on next page)

CHAPTER 4 PART 1

human (pages 92-93).

34. The student should know that INFANT chimpanzee skulls look like what adult animal as far as where the spinal cord enters (pages 92-93).

35. The student should know that the Taung Child's vertical forehead, absent eyebrow ridges, and central spinal cord opening was not proof that the Taung Child was an ape-man as Dart thought, but proof that the Taung Child was similar to an infant ape.

36. The student should know that Dr. Dart was promoted to Dean of the Faculty of Medicine at the University of the Witwatersrand after he made the Taung Child blunder (page 97).

37. The student should know what years (starting year-ending year), and the total number of years the evolution community rejected Dr. Dart's claim that the Taung Child was an ape-man (page 98).

38. The student should know that the hole in the bottom of a skull where the spinal cord enters is called the foramen magnum.

39. The student should know Dr. Dart thought blackened bones found in Makapansgat Cave South Africa was evidence of what (page 98)?

40. The student should know the fossil antelope leg bones Dr. Dart found at the Makapansgat Cave were battered on the ends (page 99). How did Dr. Dart interpret these bones?

41. The student should know that Dr. Dart found animal bones at the Makapansgat Cave that were split and crushed (page 99). How did Dr. Dart interpret these bones?

42. The student should be able to answer this: If australopithecines hunted antelope and other large animals and ate the marrow from the bones as Dr. Dart suggested, what kind of diet did they have? Vegetarian or carnivorous (page 99)?
43. The student should know that apes today are mostly vegetarian (page 102).

44. Mr. James Kitching found the first fossil of Dr. Dart's second ape-man, *Australopithecus prometheus*. What cave was it found in and what year?
The student should also know what was the fossil number was and what body part was it (page 102 top).

45. The student should know and be able to write out from memory the three evidences of the controlled use of fire Dr. Dart found at Makapansgat Cave (page 101).

46. The student should know what the Greek mythological figure Prometheus was famous for according to Greek myths (page 102).

(Continued on next page)

CHAPTER 4 PART 1

47. The student should know Dr. Dart reported he found bashed in baboon skulls at both the Makapansgat and Taung Caves. What did Dr. Dart think this meant (page 103)?

48. The student should know how bashed in baboon skulls was transformed into the script of the movie *2001: A Space Odyssey* (page 103, 120, 121).

49. The student should know that when Dr. Dart reported he found evidence that australopithecines controlled the use of fire and used bone tools (both advanced human-like behaviors), his colleagues finally relented and accepted the idea that australopithecines (both the Taung Child and *Australopithecine prometheus*) were ape-men in 1948 (page 103). This is a historic and important point that this cultural evidence is what convinced them, not the fossils!

50. The student should know the simplest ways to distinguish an ape from a human pelvis (page 107). This is also a very important point!

51. The student should know that in the human pelvis, the top edge of the ilium bone (red line page 107), called the iliac crest, starts out facing sideways and turns forward more than 90 degrees (red arrowhead).

52. The student should know that in an ape pelvis, the top edge of the ilium bone (blue line page 107), called the iliac crest, starts out facing sideways but only turns slightly forward (blue arrowhead).

53. The student should know what the fossil prefix MLD stands for (page 106).

54. The student should know what the fossil prefix MLC stands for (page 106).

55. The student should know the two pelvis bone official identification #s that Dr. Dart found. The student should know Dr. Dart placed MLD 7 and MLD 8 into a full human pelvis (page 107).

56. When Dr. Dart claimed that the pelvis of *Australopithecus prometheus* was human shaped, what did this imply about the form of locomotion of this creature (page 107)?

57. The student should know that Dart's reconstructed pelvis of *Australopithecus prometheus* looked nearly identical to a modern human pelvis (page 108).

58. The student should know that since Dart's reconstructed pelvis of *Australopithecus prometheus* looked like a modern human pelvis, this was strong evidence that this was not an ape that walked on all fours but an ape-man that walked upright like humans (page 108).

59. The student should know that the collarbone of *Australopithecus prometheus* was human shaped and this was evidence that this creature was what kind of animal (page 109).

(Continued on next page)

CHAPTER 4 PART 1

60. The student should know that Dart told *The New York Times* the skull (brain size) of *Australopithecus prometheus* was large. He said australopithecines have brains of how many cc _____ and this was equivalent in size to what animal _____ (page 116).

61. The student should know that when *The New York Times* printed that the brain size of *Australopithecus prometheus* was large, the article headline read, "Man-Ape Study Backs Theory The Missing Link _____ _____ _____" (page 116).

62. The student should know that Dr. Dart implied that not only did the infant Taung Child have a centrally located spinal cord (foramen magnum), but also the adult australopithecine, *Australopithecus prometheus* (page 117). What did this imply as to how these australopithecines walk (page 117)?

63. The student should know the name of the Hollywood movie and the name of the best selling book that were based on Dr. Dart's tool-using, fire-using, head-bashing, large-brained ape-man (page 120).

64. The student should know that when Dr. Dart's many discoveries were being heralded in science journals and newspapers throughout the world, there seemed little reason to doubt the authenticity of Dart's fire-using ape-man. But as time progressed, his scientific facts and interpretations, even his trustworthiness as a scientist, were questioned (page 121).

65. The student should know where the Taung Child was found (page 92).

66. The student should be able to write out, from memory the three human characters of the Taung Child skull and the three human characters of *Australopithecus prometheus* (see chart before question one on this Student Objectives Sheet).

67. The student should be able to fill out this chart from memory:

	Dart's <u>First</u> Ape-Man	**Dart's <u>Second</u> Ape-Man**
Year:		
Common name:	_____	_____
Location:	_____	_____

(Continued on next page)

	Dart's <u>First</u> Ape-Man	**Dart's <u>Second</u> Ape-Man**
Species name:	_____	_____
Developmental age:	_____	_____
Initial reaction:	_____	_____
Why this reaction?	_____	_____
Fossil: Human Character 1	_____	_____
Human Character 2	_____	_____
Human Character 3	_____	_____

(End Student Objectives First Half Chapter 4)

This is the back side of a student handout page.

Teacher's Notes for Week 9
Teacher time for this class: 5 minutes

TEACHER STEP 1: Read Out Loud: Because this section is so long and complicated, we are going to give you a chance to study the Student Objective Sheet today in class. You can either study on your own or break into groups of 2 students and take turns quizzing each other.

TEACHER STEP 2: READ AT END OF CLASS: Next week, at the beginning of class there will be a quiz over this Student Objective Sheet. You should study your sheet and be ready. Remember, if you study and memorize the Student Objectives Sheet, you should be able to get a 100%.

Teacher's Notes for Week 10
Teacher time for this class: 45 minutes

TEACHER STEP 3: Students take quiz. Pass out the "First Half Chapter 4 Quiz" which are on the following pages. (You can choose from one of three sample quizzes, either Quiz A, B, C.) The quiz is only 10 questions long. Grade the quizzes with the provided answer sheet (Either A, B, or C) and record the grade.

TEACHER STEP 1 Class Discussion: The teacher now reads these questions out loud. Encourage everyone to participate. After the students try to give an answer, the teacher should help them with the answer if needed.

Class Discussion Question #4. What do you do when a scientist presents compelling evidence of a theory that you do not necessarily agree? Do you accept the evidence as facts? What should you do?

Answer: You should always take the facts under advisement. Many times it takes 50 or 100 years to overturn compelling anatomical evidence of an ape-man. Piltdown took 40 years to overturn. Neanderthal Man took 70 years.

TEACHER STEP 2: To help the student consolidate this information, the students should now be offered to re-watch the DVD segment that coincides with this chapter. The DVD for this topic is entitled *Episode 3, Untold Stories of Human Evolution*. Hit "**menu**" on DVD remote. Select "**Chapters**." Hit the button next to "**Prometheus**." This segment is about 20 minutes long. Once this segment is done, the typing on the screen with keyboard sounds starts for next segment, turn off the DVD. **Don't let the student watch the whole DVD yet.** IF you have rented Episode 3 (365 day rental) from our video on demand site (https://thegrandexperiment.vhx.tv) watch segment which starts at 10 minutes 18 seconds and ends at 31 minutes.

TEACHER STEP 3: With any remaining time, students can begin to read the second half of Chapter 4, pages 121-168.

TEACHER STEP 4: There is no homework. Next week, in class, we will continue reading the second half of this chapter 4.

Name:_____   Date:_____

Quiz First Half Chapter 4
(*A. prometheus*/Ape-Man of 2001: A Space Odyssey)
Quiz A

1. What cave was *Australopithecus prometheus* found, in what country? _____
_____

2. <u>What chairmanship</u> did Dr. Dart hold and at what institution? _____
_____

3. What kind of diet did Dr. Dart think that *Australopithecus prometheus* have? Vegetarian or mostly meat-eating? _____

4. What evidence finally convinced Dr. Dart's doubting colleagues that australopithecines were ape-men? _____

5. What is the simplest way to distinguish an ape from a human pelvis? _____
_____

6. What does the fossil prefix MLD stand for? _____

7. What two pelvis bones (Fossil #) did Dr. Dart use to reconstruct the pelvis of *Australopithecus prometheus?* _____ _____

8. What was the name of the best selling <u>book</u> that was based on Dr. Dart's tool-using, fire-using, head-bashing, large-brained ape-man? _____,

9. Where the Taung Child found? Name of quarry and country. _____
_____ (page 92).

10. What animal do infant ape skulls resemble? _____

This is the back side of a student handout page.

Name:_____   Date:_____

Quiz First Half Chapter 4
(*A. prometheus*/Ape-Man of 2001: A Space Odyssey)
Quiz B

True or False:

1. An endocast is the mold of the inside of a skull. _____

2. The discovery of the Taung Child was not all that important in the big picture of science. _____

3. The formal scientific species name for the Taung Child is *Australopithecus prometheus*. _____

4. Dr. Dart's mentor, Dr. Grafton Elliot Smith, promoted three ape-men that turned out to be not ape-men. _____

5. A skull of a modern baby chimpanzee looks like the skull of an adult chimpanzee. _____

6. The evolution community rejected Dr. Dart's claim that the Taung Child was an ape-man for more than 20 years. _____

7. Dr. Dart thought the ape-man found at Makapansgat was vegetarian. _____

8. In an ape pelvis, the top edge of the ilium bone called the iliac crest, starts out facing sideways and turns forward more than 90 degrees. _____

9. When Dr. Dart's announced many discoveries about the controlled use of fire and bone tools used by *Australopithecus prometheus*, there seemed little reason to doubt the authenticity of Dart's fire-using, bone-tool using ape-man. _____

10. The Neanderthal ape-man, heavily endorsed by Dr. Grafton Elliot Smith turned out to be an ape. _____

This is the back side of a student handout page.

Name:_____   Date:_____

Quiz First Half Chapter 4
(*A. prometheus*/Ape-Man of 2001: A Space Odyssey)
Quiz C

Answer the following:

1. What cave was *Australopithecus prometheus* found, in what country? _____
_____

2. *Modern baby ape* skulls look similar to what adult animal skull?_____

3. What year was the Taung Child discovered and what year was the first *Australopithecus prometheus* found? _____   _____

4. Dr. Dart thought blackened bones found in Makapansgat Cave South Africa was evidence of what? _____

4. What evidence finally convinced Dr. Dart's doubting colleagues that australopithecines were ape-men? _____

5. What were the three evidences that *Australopithecus prometheus* used and controlled the use of fire? _____   _____   _____

6. Dart's reconstructed pelvis of *Australopithecus prometheus* looked nearly identical to the pelvis of what animal? _____

7. Dart told *The New York Times* the brain size of australopithecines were how large (in cc) and equivalent in size to what animal brain? _____ cc _____.

8. What was the name of the Hollywood movie that was based on Dr. Dart's tool-using, fire-using, head-bashing, large-brained ape-man? _____

9. Name the three ape-men endorsed by Dr. Grafton Elliot Smith which turned out to be NOT ape-men. _____   _____
_____

10. According to Dr. Dart, the *Australopithecus prometheus* collarbone looked similar to the collarbone of what type of animal? _____

This is the back side of a student handout page.

Answers Quiz A
Quiz First Half Chapter 4
(*A. prometheus*/Ape-Man of 2001: A Space Odyssey)

1. Makapansgat Cave, South Africa. (Must name both to get correct.)
2. Chairman of Anatomy University of the Witwatersrand.
3. Mostly meat eating or carnivorous
4. controlled the use of fire and tools (page 103)
5. How much top edge of the ilium bone, called the iliac crest, turns forward. (page 107)
6. <u>M</u>akapansgat <u>L</u>imeworks <u>D</u>ump (page 106)
7. MLD 7 and MLD 8
8. African Genesis (page 120)
9. Taung, South Africa
10. Adult human skulls

Answers Quiz B
Quiz First Half Chapter 4
(*A. prometheus*/Ape-Man of 2001: A Space Odyssey)

1. True
2. False
3. False (*Australopithecus africanus*)
4. True
5. False.
6. True (1925-1948 page 98)
7. False
8. False (human pelvis turns forward 90 degrees, an ape pelvis only turns slightly forward)
9. True
10. False (It turned out to be a human)

ANSWER SHEETS

Answers Quiz C
Quiz First Half Chapter 4
(*A. prometheus*/Ape-Man of 2001: A Space Odyssey)

1. Makapansgat Cave, South Africa

2. (modern) adult human

3. 1924 (page 92) 1947 (page 102)

4. evidence of the controlled the use of fire and tools (page 103)

5. fire hearths, ash, burned bones

6. human (page 108)

7. 1000 cc, human (page 116)

8. *2001: A Space Odyssey* (page 120)

9. Piltdown man
    Neanderthal Man
    Nebraska Man (or *Hesperopithecus*)

10. human

Teacher's Notes for Week 11
Teacher time for this class: 5 minutes

TEACHER STEP 1: Read out loud: Today in class, you are to finish reading the second half of Chapter 4, pages 121-168. If you don't finish reading in class you are to read at home for homework. No quiz next week.

Teacher's Notes for Week 12
Teacher time for this class: 5 minutes

TEACHER STEP 1:

Read out loud: Today in class, you are to fill out the Student Objective Sheet for Second Half of Chapter 4. What you don't finish reading in class you are to finish at home for homework then study for quiz for next class. REMEMBER, A QUIZ NEXT WEEK AT BEGINNING OF CLASS.

Pass out Student Objective Sheet for the second half of Chapter 4 (next pages).

CHAPTER 4 PART 2

Student Objectives Sheet for Second Half of Chapter 4 (Pages 121-168)

By studying these objectives and knowing this core information, you should be able to pass the quiz at the beginning of class next week.

The student should know that Dr. Dart basically found two ape-men. It is imperative that the student not get these two ape-men confused. The first was The Taung Child *Australopithecus africanus* found in 1924. The second ape-man was the adult fire-using, bone-tool using Prometheus, *Australopithecus prometheus* found in 1947. The student should be able to recreate this chart below from memory. You will see that many of the student objectives can be answered from this chart:

	Dart's First Ape-Man	Dart's Second Ape-Man
Year:	1924/1925	1947
Common name/nickname:	Taung Child	Prometheus
Location:	Taung Quarry, South Africa	Makapansgat Cave, South Africa
Species name:	*Australopithecus africanus*	*Australopithecus prometheus*
Developmental age:	Child	Adult
Initial reaction:	Initially rejected by scientists	Initially accepted by scientists
Why this reaction?	Infant ape skulls look like humans	Found with fire and tools
Fossil:	Face/front skull/endocast	MLD 1 Skull fragment + others
Human Character 1	Flat vertical face	Human-shaped pelvis
Human Character 2	No eyebrow ridges	Human-shaped collarbone
Human Character 3	Forward positioned spinal cord	Human-sized brain, 1000 cc

1. The student should know the nickname (page 92), the formal species name (two Latin names for genus and species page 92) and the year discovered (page 92) of the first ape-man that Dr. Dart promoted.

2. The student should know the nickname (Prometheus), the formal species name (two Latin names for genus and species page 102 bottom) and the year first fossil discovered (page 102) of the second ape-man that Dr. Dart promoted to the world as an ape-man.

3. The student should know that Dr. Dart had to retract the first skull of *Australopithecus prometheus* that he submitted to *Nature*. The first *Australopithecus prometheus* skull he submitted turned out to be what kind of animal (page 122)?

4. The student should know why Dr. Dart hurriedly sent a telegram to the editors of *Nature* instructing them not to publish the article he had just sent (page 122).

5. The student should know WHEN Dr. Dart's colleagues disclosed Dr. Dart's mistake

(Continued on next page)

CHAPTER 4 PART 2

of submitting a baboon skull to *Nature*. <u>Not</u> the year but when in relation to Dr. Dart's career/life (bottom of page 122).

6. The student should know if a baboon is a monkey or an ape (page 123 bottom).

7. The student should know if a chimpanzee is a monkey or an ape (page 123 bottom).

8. The student should be able to write out, from memory, the four types of apes living today, and divide them into the <u>great apes</u> and <u>lesser apes</u>. Important.
Great Apes living today: Chimp, gorilla, orangutan
Lesser Ape living today: Gibbon

9. The student should know the relative size of a baboon skull (brain) as compared to a chimp skull (brain) (page 123 bottom).

10. The student should know and reflect upon the fact that although Dr. Dart had a prestigious title in anatomy (Chairman of Anatomy at the University of the Witwatersrand), he was unable to distinguish a monkey skull from an ape skull.

11. The student should be able to write out the four evidences of the controlled use of fire at Makapansgat that Dr. Dart presented (page 124).

12. The student should know that Dr. Dart had the black bones from Makapansgat tested positive for the residues of fire twice (1926 and 1946) and both times the chemists concluded the bones were blackened by fire (pages 98, 99, and top page 124).

13. The student should know that later, an independent scientist not working with Dr. Dart, Dr. Kenneth Oakley, retested the black bones from Makapansgat and determined the black color was not from fire but what (page 124)?

14. The student should know where the iron and manganese that stained the animal bones black in the Makapansgat Cave came from (page 124).

15. The student should know that once the controlled use of fire was disproved at Makapansgat, Dr. Oakley suggested that *Australopithecus prometheus* was more like an animal than a man (page 124 bottom).

16. The student should know that Dr. Oakley determined that the black carbon on the surface of Dr. Dart's fossil bones was not from the controlled use of fire but from what source (page 124 bottom)?

17. The student should know that Dr. Dart said *Australopithecus prometheus* used bone tools to kill three types of animals. What were the three types of animals (126 top)?

18. The student should know the name (write out from memory) for the type of bone

(Continued on next page)

CHAPTER 4 PART 2

tools he found at Makapansgat and the acronym he came up with (page 111 bottom).

19. The student should know that, according to Dr. Dart, ODK ape-man tools were from three different parts of an animal's skeleton. Name these three parts and how these three parts make up the acronym ODK (page 111 bottom).

20. The student should know what important award did Dr. Dart receive from the Wenner-Gren Foundation in New York after releasing his book on ODK ape-man tools (page 118 and page 126 bottom right).

21. The student should know that Dr. Charles K. (Bob) Brain demonstrated that Dr. Dart's ape-man ODK clubs were actually similar to goat bones chewed by dogs (pages 128-129).

22. The student should know how many ape-man stone tools were collected at Makapansgat by Dart's associates and how many of these were later determined to be just ordinary rocks (page 132 bottom). Important: This is stone tools now, not the ODK bone tools.

23. The student should know Dr. Dart's team found a second ape-man at Makapansgat, an *Australopithecus prometheus* upper jaw fossil (fossil # MLC 1), found next to pebbles. The student should know Dr. Dart thought this was evidence that *Australopithecus prometheus* used stone pebbles as rudimentary tools.

24. The student should know that fossil MLC 1 turned out to be a _____ jaw (page 134 bottom).

25. All five experts (Alun Hughes, Revil Mason, 'Bob' Brain, Brian Maguire, Professor C. van Riet Lowe and Dr. Dart) who were dealing with the anthropological evidence at Makapansgat (fire residue, stone tools and bone tools), had one thing in common. The student should know what they had in common (page 135).

26. The student should know that the Taung Child (*Australopithecus africanus*), Prometheus (*Australopithecus prometheus*), and the nearly complete skull found by Dr. Broom which he named Mrs. Ples (*Plesianthropus transvaalensis*), *all* turned out to be the same species (page 136). What species were they? THIS IS VERY IMPORTANT

27. Next the student should be able to fill out this chart from memory: IMPORTANT:

FOSSIL	INITIAL SPECIES NAME	TRUE SPECIES NAME
Taung Child:	_____ _____	_____ _____
Prometheus:	_____ _____	_____ _____
Mrs. Ples:	_____ _____	_____ _____

28. The student should know that Dr. Dart falsely inflated the brain size of the Taung

(Continued on next page)

Child to make it look more like an ape-man. By how much (%) did he falsely increase the Taung Child skull size (page 137)?

29. The student should know that Dr. Dart inflated the brain size of the fossil skull MLD 1, bigger than it actually was, to make it look more like an ape-man. By how much (%) did he falsely increase the skull MLD 1 (page 138)?

30. The student should know that Dr. Dart reconstructed the *Australopithecus prometheus* skull fragments found at Makapansgat to look like an ape-man with a human flat face. In reality, since *Australopithecus prometheus* is *Australopithecus africanus,* it should look like the complete *Australopithecus africanus* skull Mrs. Ples, and Mrs. Ples has a protuberant face (muzzle) like a chimpanzee (page 139).

31. The student should know the name of the large opening in the base of the skull, through which the spinal cord enters (page 140).

32. The student should know if the foramen magnum of Mrs. Ples (an adult *Australopithecus africanus*) is in the back of the skull like a chimpanzee or in the center of the bottom of the skull like a human (see photos at bottom of page 140).

33. The student should know that since the foramen magnum of the complete skull Mrs. Ples (an adult *Australopithecus africanus*) is in the back of the skull (like a chimpanzee), then in reality the foramen magnum for the Taung Child (*Australopithecus africanus*) would be in the same position (in the back of the skull like a chimpanzee) once the Taung Child reached maturity.

34. The student should know that since the foramen magnum of the complete and reliable skull Mrs. Ples (an adult *Australopithecus africanus*) is in the back of the skull (like a chimpanzee) then the foramen magnum for Prometheus (which was renamed *Australopithecus africanus* and is an adult *Australopithecus africanus*) would also be in the back of the skull like a chimpanzee, not in the middle of the bottom of the skull like Dr. Dart claimed.

35. The student should be able to fill out a chart like this from memory:

	Dart's Initial Foramen Magnum Claim	Reality
1924 Taung Child	Foramen Magnum in human position	In back, in ape position
1947 Makapansgat	Foramen Magnum in human position	In back, in ape position
1947 Mrs. Ples		In back, in ape position

36. The student should know that according to Dr. Dart, the position of the foramen magnum coincides with how an animal walks. If the foramen magnum is in the back of the skull like a chimpanzee, then the animal walks on all fours (quadruped). If the foramen magnum is in the center of the bottom of the skull, like a human, then the animal

(Continued on next page)

CHAPTER 4 PART 2

walks erect on two feet (bipedal). Using this information and the information in the chart above, how did the Taung child, Prometheus and Mrs. Ples walk? On all fours like an ape, or upright like Dr. Dart suggested (page 140)?

37. The student should know that Dr. Dart falsely inserted the two small pelvis bones he found at Makapansgat (MLD 7 and MLD 8) into a complete human pelvis and then claimed this proved that this creature had a human-shaped pelvis and walked upright like a human. In reality the reconstructed pelvis should have looked like Mrs. Ples pelvis which is flat, like a chimpanzee (page 142-145).

38. The student should know that the upper blade of a chimpanzee pelvis and the upper blade of an *Australopithecus africanus* pelvis (Prometheus, Mrs. Ples, Taung Child) do not turn forward 90 degrees as in humans (page 145). This implies all of these animals walked on all fours.

39. The student should know that Dr. Dart found thousands of animal bones in the caves of Makapansgat. From this, he falsely believed the australopithecines lived in the caves and were big game hunters, eating their kill in the caves, and roasting their kill over fires. In reality, the australopithecines were not the hunters but the _____ and were brought there as kill by leopards and other animals (pages 146-151).

40. The student should be able to write out <u>from memory</u> the six types of bones Dr. Dart used to create his famous ape-man from Makapansgat *Australopithecus prometheus*: 1) canid (dog family), 2) baboon (monkey), 3) bovid (cattle family), 4) horse (horse family), 5) feline (cat family) and 6) *Australopithecus africanus* bones (pages 154-155).

41. The student should know that Dr. Dart created the ape-man from Makapansgat Cave using bones from how many different types of <u>NON-Primate</u> animal bones (pages 154-155)? (1) canid (dog family), 2) baboon (monkey), 3) bovid (cattle family), 4) horse (horse family), 5) feline (cat family) see above.

42. The student should know that Dr. Dart lied when he said he never claimed the Taung Child was a missing link (page 159).

43. The student should know that Dr. Dart lied when he said he never claimed the Taung Child was a missing link. What other famous scientist denied he had called his ape-man fossil an ape-man (page 159)?

44. The student should know that many of Dr. Dart's colleagues including Dr. Brain (page 126 and 159), Dr. Ron Clarke, Dr. Stringer (page 138), Dr. Oakley (page 126), Dr. Le Gros Clark (page 126), felt that Dr. Dart was more of a big story teller, rather than "one of the great scholar-scientists of the era" (page 90).

45. The student should be able to write out Dr. Dart's 12 word quote which indicated he

(Continued on next page)

was willing to make up stories about ape-men. IMPORTANT "Never let the _____
_____" (page 160).

46. The student should know that the ape-man from Makapansgat, *Australopithecus prometheus*, was assigned six different ages ranging from 150,000 years old to 3.7 million years old (page 164).

(End Student Objectives Sheet for Second Half of Chapter 4)

Teacher's Notes for Week 13
Teacher time for this class: 40 minutes

TEACHER STEP 1: Students take quiz. Pass out the "Second Half Chapter 4 Quiz" which are on the following pages. (You can choose from one of three sample quizzes, either Quiz A, B, C.) The quiz is only 10 questions long. Grade the quiz with the provided answer sheet (Either A, B, or C) and record the grade.

Next Chapter: Chapter 5 The Orce Ape-Man

TEACHER STEP 2: Next the students should watch the DVD segment that coincides with Chapter 5, The Orce Ape-Man. Start the DVD entitled, *Episode 3, Untold Stories of Human Evolution,* at the very beginning by pressing the button "**Play**." When the Orce Ape-Man segment ends (at about 13 minutes), turn off the DVD. You can tell when a segment has ended when the screen turns to black then keyboard typing begins on screen for the next segment. **Don't let the student watch the whole DVD yet.**
IF you have rented Episode 3 (365 day rental) from our video on demand site (https://thegrandexperiment.vhx.tv) simply watch the first 13 minutes of the video. (Turn off when the screen turns to black then keyboard typing begins on screen for the next segment.)

TEACHER STEP 3 Class Discussion about DVD:

Class Discussion Question #1. Do you think the Orce Museum should remove the Orce ape-man display since the Orce Man skull since this has been shown to be the skull of a donkey?

Answer: Let the students answer.

Class Discussion Question #2. Do you think scientists should stop writing books and science articles about ape-men from Orce given the fact that the Orce ape-man turned out to be a donkey skull, a ruminant leg bone, and a hippo tooth?

Answer: Let the students answer.

TEACHER STEP 4: READ OUT LOUD: For the rest of class, read Chapter 5, The Orce Ape-Man. It is a bit shorter, only 37 pages. Your homework tonight is to finish reading this chapter on your own. No quiz next week.

(End Teacher's Note Week 13)

This is the back side of a teacher's page.

Name:_____   Date:_____

Quiz Second Half Chapter 4
(*A. prometheus*/Ape-Man of 2001: A Space Odyssey)
Quiz A

Answer the following:

1. What it the formal species names that Dr. Dart <u>initially</u> assigned to his first ape-man discovered in 1924 and Dr. Dart initially assigned to the second ape-man fossil discovered in 1947?
    1924: _____
    1947: _____

2. Dr. Dart quickly retracted the first skull of *Australopithecus prometheus* that he submitted to *Nature*. What kind of animal was it that Dart retracted it? _____

3. When Dr. Kenneth Oakley retested the black bones from Makapansgat he determined the black color was not from the controlled use of fire but was from <u>elements</u> that had dripped from the cave ceiling onto the bones in the cave. What were the two elements that turned the bones black? _____ _____

4. ODK bone tool culture is an acronym for ape-man bone tools found at Makapansgat. Write out the full name for ODK. _____

5. Prometheus and Mrs. Ples were given the wrong species names initially. What species did they both turn out to be? _____

6. Is the foramen magnum of an <u>adult</u> *Australopithecus africanus* in the back of the base of the skull like a chimpanzee or in the center of the base of the skull like a human?
_____

7. Does the upper blade of the pelvis of *Australopithecus africanus* look like a human pelvis or a chimp pelvis? _____

8. Dr. Dart falsely believed the australopithecines lived in the caves and were big game hunters. In reality, australopithecines were the _____.

9/10. Dr. Dart mixed many types of animal bones together to make up his ape-man *Australopithecus prometheus*. Besides *Australopithecus* bones and baboon bones, name two other types of animal bones he used?

9. _____

10. _____

This is the back side of a student handout page.

Name:_____   Date:_____

Quiz Second Half Chapter 4
(*A. prometheus*/Ape-Man of 2001: A Space Odyssey)
Quiz B

True or False:

1. A baboon is a monkey. _____

2. A baboon skull is larger than a chimpanzee skull. _____

3. All four of Dr. Dart's evidences for the controlled use of fire at Makapansgat turned out to be accurate._____

4. At Makapansgat, Dr. Dart's team collected a total of 2400 rocks that they claimed were "stone tools." _____

5. The five experts who were dealing with the anthropological evidence at Makapansgat (stone tools, bone tools, and the evidence of fire) did not have a Ph.D. in anthropology or archaeology. _____

6. The Taung Child, Prometheus, and Mrs. Ples turned out to be the same species. _____

7. Dr. Dart falsely inserted the two small pelvis bones he found at Makapansgat (MLD 7 and MLD 8) into a complete human pelvis and then claimed this proved that this creature walked upright like a human. _____

8. Dr. Dart lied and said he never claimed the Taung Child was a missing link. _____

9. Dr. Dart created the ape-man from Makapansgat using the bones of fourteen different types of animals. _____

10. Write out Dr. Dart's 12 word quote which he privately told a colleague that indicates he was willing to make up stories about ape-men. "Never _____
_____

This is the back side of a student handout page.

CHAPTER 4 PART 2

Name:_____   Date:_____

Quiz Second Half Chapter 4
(*A. prometheus*/Ape-Man of 2001: A Space Odyssey)
Quiz C

Answer the following:

1. What it the <u>nickname</u> (common name) for Dr. Dart's first ape-man discovered in 1924 and the nickname for Dr. Dart's second ape-man fossil discovered in 1947?
    1924:_____
    1947:_____

2. What are the three types great apes living today? _____ _____ _____

3. What are the four evidences of the controlled use of fire at Makapansgat that Dr. Dart presented?
_____ _____ _____ _____

4. Dr. Charles K. (Bob) Brain demonstrated that Dr. Dart's ape-man clubs were actually similar to what type of modern animal bones? _____

5. Write out Dr. Dart's 12 word quote which indicated he was willing to make up stories about ape-men. "Never _____
_____

6. How many different ages did scientists assign the fossils at Makapansgat cave?

7. Dr. Charles K. (Bob) Brain demonstrated that Dr. Dart's australopithecine bones did not get to the caves because they lived in the cave but they were brought to the cave by _____.

Matching. Place the letter A or B next to each pelvis

8. Human pelvis _____   A. Upper pelvis turns forward 90 degrees

9. Ape pelvis _____   B. Upper pelvis goes out sideways

10. *Australopithecus* pelvis_____

This is the back side of a student handout page.

(Continued on next page)

CHAPTER 4 PART 2

Answers Quiz A
Second First Half of Chapter 4
(*A. prometheus*/Ape-Man of 2001: A Space Odyssey)

1. Must get both answer right to get a right answer:

    1924: *Australopithecus africanus*

    1947: *Australopithecus prometheus*

2. Baboon

3. iron and manganese (page 124)

4. Osteodontokeratic

5. *Australopithecus africanus*

6. Back (like a chimp)

7. Chimp

8. were the hunted (or were brought there by other animals such as leopards, hyenas, eagles etc.)

For 9 and 10, any one of these animals counts as a right answer (pages 154-155).

    canid (dog family)

    bovid (cattle family)

    horse (horse family)

    feline (cat family)

9. (see above)

10. (see above)

Answers Quiz B
Second Half of Chapter 4
(*A. prometheus*/Ape-Man of 2001: A Space Odyssey)

1. True

2. False

3. False

4. False

5. True

6. True

7. True

8. True

9. False, the ape-man was made using the bones of 6 different types of animals (pages 154-155).

10. "Never let the truth get in the way of a good story"

Answers Quiz C
Second First Half of Chapter 4
(*A. prometheus*/Ape-Man of 2001: A Space Odyssey)

1. Taung Child, Prometheus

2. Chimpanzee, gorilla, orangutan

3. Burned trees, fire hearths (or hearths), ash like material (or breccia), black (or charred) bones, (124 top).

4. goat bones or goat bones chewed by dogs (pages 128-129).

5. "Never let the truth get in the way of a good story"

6. six (page 164 right)

7. leopards (or animals or hyenas or eagles, or porcupines) (pages 146-151)

8. A

9. B

10. B

Teacher's Notes for Week 14
Teacher time for this class: 10 minutes

TEACHER STEP 1: Pass out the Student Objectives Sheets for Chapter 5, The Orce Ape-Man (pages that follow) at the beginning of class. Tell the students that they should work on them in class. What they do not finish they can finish as homework. <u>At the beginning of class next week there will be a quiz on the Orce Ape-Man.</u>

This is the back side of a teacher page.

CHAPTER 5

Student Objectives Sheet for Chapter 5
The Orce Ape-Man (5 pages)

By studying these objectives and knowing this core information, you should be able to pass the quiz at the beginning of class next week.

1. The student should know that Dr. Miquel Crusafont was one of the leading paleontologists of the twentieth century (page 170).

2. The student should know that the leading evolution scientists keep making big mistakes:
Dr. Florentino Ameghino, the most famous scientist in South America: raccoon-man.
Dr. Henry Fairfield Osborn, the most famous scientist in North America: pig-man.
Dr. Miquel Crusafont, the leading paleontologist in Europe: donkey-man.

3. The student should know that Dr. Miquel Crusafont was known for directing the team of paleontologists who discovered the oldest ape-man ever found in Europe and Asia—the Orce Ape-Man.

4. The student should know that the first Orce Man fossil, a skull piece, was discovered in August 1982 and Dr. Crusafont died of throat cancer one year later in August 1983 (page 170 and 172).

5. The student should know the name of the research organization/museum that Dr. Miquel Crusafont founded and directed, including the abbreviation for this same research organization/museum (page 171).

6. The student should know who took over directing the ICP research organization/museum and the Orce dig when Dr. Crusafont died in August 1983 (page 172).

7. The student should know from memory the year the Orce ape-man skull was found, when it was announced, and when the inside surface of the fossil was finally exposed.

Orce ape-man skull was found	1982
Orce ape-man skull announced	1983
Orce ape-man skull cleaned	1984

8. The student should know what was so important about the Orce Ape-Man skull that caused the small town of Orce, Spain to become a science tourism destination (page 172).

9. The student should know there are three dig sites near Orce where this "ape-man" and his stone "tools" were found (pages 175, 176, 177).

(Continued on next page)

CHAPTER 5

10. The student should be able to write out from memory the names of the three dig sites in Orce (pages 175, 176, 177).

11. The student should know which of the dig sites near Orce where the Orce-Ape Man skull was found (page 175).

12. There were three ape-man bones found at the Venta Micena dig site near Orce, Spain. The student should know what body parts each of these three ape-man fossils were (page 175).

13. The student should know the name of the second dig site near Orce where two different teeth were found. The student should also know what kind of teeth the team of scientists working in Orce thought the two teeth were (page 176).

14. The student should know that today the majority of evolution scientists no longer believe the Orce Man skull, arm bones and tooth are from an ape-man but from what kind of animals (page 178).

15. The student should know that many scientists think the three Orce Ape-man bones and the tooth are not even from primates (page 178).

16. The student should know that even though the majority of scientists do not think the three Orce bones and the tooth are from primates, the Orce Man museum still displays the Orce skull as an ape-man skull and the rocks found nearby as "stone tools" (page 178).

17. The student should know that when the Orce ape-man skull was found at the Venta Micena dig site, the outside surface was easily viewable but the inside surface was covered with sediment (see pictures top of page 179).

18. The student should know that when the scientists announced they had found an ape-man at Orce they still had not removed the sediment yet (page 182).

19. The student should know what age of an individual the Orce ape-man fossil skull was (according to scientists talking to reporters at the first press conference) (page 180).

20. The student should know the scientists described the Orce ape-man skull as an ape-man partway evolved between what two other ape-men (page 180). IMPORTANT.

21. The student should know how many news articles were published about the Orce ape-man in the first year after it was announced (page 180).

22. The student should know that scientists described the Orce ape-man in their first press conference as arguably the oldest ape-man (hominid) ever found in Europe or Asia (page 180 newspaper article bottom right).

(Continued on next page)

CHAPTER 5

23. The student should know the year the cement-like sediment was finally removed from the inside of the skull (page 180).

24. The student should know <u>when</u> the cement-like sediment was removed from the inside of the Orce ape-man skull (in relation to the announcement that scientists had found an ape-man skull) (page 180).

25. The student should know the definition of a skull suture line (page 180).

26. The student should know that when the inside of the Orce ape-man skull was cleaned, two unexpected findings were discovered which suggested the skull was not a primate (page 182). From memory, what are these two findings?

27. The student should be able to identify the Orce skull abnormally wavy suture line and large crest from a picture (right) (page 182).

28. The student should know the unusual large crest on the Orce skull suggests it is not a primate but of the horse family (page 182).

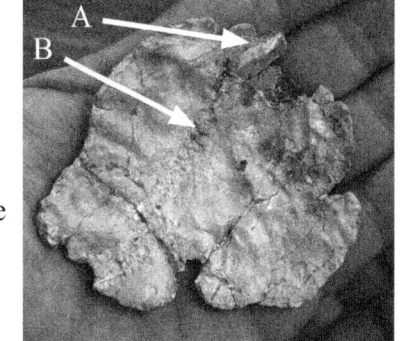

29. The student should know the horse family, Equidae, includes: horses, asses (donkeys), and zebras.

30. The student should know that when Dr. Marie de Lumley saw the inside of the skull fully exposed for the first time and saw an unusual large crest and unusual wavy suture line, she said it was what kind of animal (page 182).

31. The student should be able to write out, from memory, the six different opinions evolution scientists have rendered as to what the Orce skull actually was (pages 184-185).

32. The student should be able to write out, from memory, the <u>three</u> different opinions evolution scientists have rendered as to what mammal <u>Order</u> the Orce skull actually was (page 185).

33. The student should know that Dr. Bienvenido Martínez and Dr. José Gibert promoted the Orce infant ape-man upper arm bone (humerus). What part of the anatomy of what kind of an animal does Dr. Bienvenido Martínez now think it is (page 186)?

34. The student should know the prefix scientists assign to any fossils or stone tools found at the Barranco León dig site near Orce (page 176).

35. The student should know that six scientists working in Orce thought the fossil tooth BL5-0 was from an ape-man, but now, other scientists think it is from what kind of animal (page 189)?

(Continued on next page)

CHAPTER 5

36. The student should know Dr. Palmqvist (Dr. José Gibert's close colleague) told reporters Dr. José Gibert had carried out a scientific fraud similar to what other famous fraud (page 191)?

37. The student should be able to write, from memory, four ape-men frauds (*Tetraprothomo* recently buried, unfossilized human bone falsely reported to be found in "rock" by Dr. Ameghino Chapter 2 page 19, Nebraska ape-man pig tooth look-alike situation that 3 scientists were aware of but did not disclose Chapter 3 page 81, Piltdown fake ape-man created by scientist at the Natural History Museum of London from an orangutan/human bones Chapter 4 page 91, Orce Ape-Man suture line manipulation by Dr. Gibert Chapter 5 page 191).

38. The student should know what was the Piltdown fraud (Piltdown fake ape-man created by scientist at the Natural History Museum of London from an orangutan/human bones Chapter 4 page 91).

39. The student should know Dr. Palmqvist accused Dr. Gibert of supplying him an oversimplified drawing of the suture line of the Orce skull for computer analysis, to make the Orce skull appear as a primate skull (page 191).

40. The student should know which of these two skull suture drawings is the one that Dr. Gibert fraudulently supplied to Dr. Palmqvist (page 191).

41. The student should know that Dr. Luis Gibert, who had worked with his father Dr. José Gibert at the Orce dig since childhood, reported that "*sometimes there are no differences*" between the "*stone tools*" found at the Orce dig sites and random rocks found along the roads in Orce (page 192).

42. The student should render an opinion if the Orce ape-man "stone tools" seen on page 193 look like stone tools or if they look like ordinary rocks.

43. The student should know that despite the 1984 revelation that the Orce ape-man skull was from a baby ass, Dr. José Gibert conducted a worldwide science publicity campaign for the next 23 years (until his death in 2007), to ensure scientific acceptance and financial support of his work.

44. The student should know that despite the 1984 revelation that the Orce ape-man skull was from a baby ass, Dr. José Gibert released his new book (*Man from Orce: The Hominids Who Came from the South*) promoting the ape-man from Orce (right). What year was this book published (page 197)?

(Continued on next page)

98

CHAPTER 5

45. The student should know that Dr. José Gibert, the primary scientist at Orce after Dr. Crusafont died, sought out and obtained endorsements from three high profile scientists regarding the authenticity of the Orce ape-man skull (donkey) and arm bones (ruminants). Write out FROM MEMORY the names of these three scientists who endorsed the Orce ape-man and what they were famous for (page 195). Important.

_____
_____
_____

46. The student should know that artistic drawings of ape-men are not evidence but are what (page 202)?

47. The student should know how many "stone tools" were collected at Orce (page 203).

48. The student should know that stone tools should be considered tentative or presumptive evidence unless they are clearly what (page 203)?

49. The student should know how many times the age of the Orce ape-man changed (page 204).

50. The student should know two examples of evolution scientists picking up random rocks and claiming they were ape-man stone tools (Chapter 4 page 168). Be able to name the location where they found their "ape-man" stone tools (random rocks).

51. Scientists initially calculated the brain size of the Orce ape-man to be how many cc and how big as compared to a human (page 170).

52. The student should know that in reality, the Orce skull was from an ass or horse, therefore was only _____ cc and was how big as compared to a human (page 199).

53. The student should be able to recreate this chart below from memory.

	INITIAL CLAIM	REALITY
Orce Skull	Human size 1,100 - 1,600 cc	Donkey size 405 - 635 cc

54. The student should know that Lemurs, monkeys, and apes belong to the mammal order Primates.

(End of Student Objectives Chapter 5)

This is the back side of a student handout page.

Teacher's Notes for Week 14
Teacher time for this class: 50 minutes

TEACHER STEP 1: Students take quiz. Pass out the "Chapter 5 Orce Ape-Man Quiz" which are on the following pages. (You can choose from one of three sample quizzes, either Quiz A, B, C.) The quiz is only 10 questions long. Grade the quiz with the provided answer sheet (Either A, B, or C) and record the grade.

Next Chapter: Chapter 6 The Libyan Ape-Man

TEACHER STEP 2: Lead class in class discussion.

Class Discussion Question #1. Is it true that scientists that believe that humans evolved from apes are smart and highly trained? Doesn't that mean that they are right?

Answer: (Students should try to answer on their own.) Even the smartest or best trained scientist can make big mistakes.

Class Discussion Question #2. Have you ever heard of a smart and highly trained scientist identifying a fossil bone as the wrong body part? (Such as a toe bone for a nose bone or an arm bone for a leg bone, etc.) Give me as many examples as you can think of including the 3 examples discussed in this book. Think hard. (Students should try to answer on their own.)

Answer:
- The Orce ape-man scientists identified a lower leg bone of a ruminant as an upper arm bone (humerus) of an ape-man.
- The highly trained tooth specialists that identified a premolar pig tooth as a molar (*not* premolar) primate tooth of Nebraska ape-man.
- The scientists that identified two horse toe bones as an ape-man collar bones on the ape-man from Makapansgat, *Australopithecus prometheus* (page 155).

Class Discussion Question #3. Do you think it is possible for a really smart and highly trained evolution scientist to identify a member of the whale family as an ape-man? (Students should try to answer on their own.)

Answer: To get the answer, you have to watch the next video segment.

TEACHER STEP 3: Next the students should watch the DVD segment that coincides with Chapter 6, The Libyan Ape-Man. This segment is on DVD entitled *"Episode 3, Untold Stories of Human Evolution."* Insert the DVD into player. When first screen comes on, press the button "**Chapters**." Then press the button "**The Libyan Ape-Man**." The segment is about 9 minutes long. Turn off the DVD when the Libyan Ape-Man segment is finished. You can tell when a segment has ended when the screen turns to black then keyboard typing begins on screen for the next segment. **Don't let the student watch the whole DVD yet.** IF you have rented Episode 3 (365 day rental) from our video on demand site (https://thegrandexperiment.vhx.tv) watch segment which starts at 31 minutes and ends when screen turns to black at 39 minutes 39 seconds.

TEACHER STEP 4: Students now begin to read in class Chapter 6 The Libyan Hominid (The Ape-Man That Challenged Lucy). It is 32 pages long.

TEACHER STEP 5: END OF CLASS THE TEACHER READS OUT LOUD: For your homework, finish reading Chapter 6, The Libyan Ape-Man. Next week in class you will fill out the Student Objective Sheet for Chapter 6. No quiz next week.

Name:_____   Date:_____

Chapter 5
The Orce Ape-Man
Quiz A

Answer the following:

1. Three ape-man fossils were found near Orce, Spain at the Venta Micena dig site. What body parts were these? _____ _____ _____

2. Scientists described the Orce ape-man skull to reporters at the press conference in 1983 as an ape-man partway evolved between what two other ape-men?
_____ _____

3. Name three animal groups that are primates. _____ _____
_____

4. When Dr. Marie de Lumley saw the inside of the Orce skull fully exposed for the first time, she saw features A and B (right) and said it was what kind of animal?

5. What would you call the unusual feature A in the picture right? _____

6. What would you call the unusual feature B in the picture right? _____

7. Evolution scientists have interpreted the Orce skull six different ways over the years. Name three of these interpretations. _____
_____ _____

8-10. Name three high profile scientists that endorsed the Orce man and what they were famous for:

Scientist: _____   Famous for: _____

Scientist: _____   Famous for: _____

Scientist: _____   Famous for: _____

This is the back side of a student handout page.

Name:_____   Date:_____

Chapter 5
The Orce Ape-Man
Quiz B

True or False:

1. Dr. Miquel Crusafont was the most important figure in Spanish Palaeontology of the twentieth century and directed the Orce man dig until his untimely death in 1983. _____

2. The Orce ape-man skull was initially thought to be the oldest ape-man ever to be discovered in Europe and Asia. _____

3. Even though the majority of evolution scientists do not think the Orce ape-man is even a primate, the "Orce ape-man skull" and the "Orce ape-man stone tools" are currently on display at a science museum in Spain. _____

4. When the Orce ape-man skull was found at the Venta Micena dig site, both surfaces were easily viewable. _____

5. Lemurs, monkeys, and apes belong to the mammal order Primates. _____

6. Evolution scientists first thought the bone found in Orce was an ape-man humerus. Now Dr. Bienvenido Martínez believes it is an elephant leg bone. _____

7. Dr. José Gibert, the lead scientist for the Orce team who took over for Dr. Crusafont after he died, was accused of fraud. _____

8. Even after the 1984 revelation that the Orce ape-man skull was from a baby ass, scientists continue to promote the skull as an ape-man. _____

9. Scientists found 6 stone tools at the Orce ape-man dig sites. _____

10. Evolution scientists *initially* claimed the Orce ape-man skull was large, more than 1,000 cc, the same size as a human skull. _____

This is the back side of a student handout page.

Name:_____   Date:_____

Chapter 5
The Orce Ape-Man
Quiz C

Answer the following:

1. How many news articles were published about the Orce ape-man in the first year alone? _____

2. What is a skull suture line? _____

3. When the inside of the Orce skull was finally cleaned, what two features were found which suggested the skull was not a primate skull.

4. Dr. Gibert was accused of fraud for supplying a fraudulent drawing of the Orce man suture line. Which of these drawings did he supply, A or B? _____

List four fraudulent ape-man:

5. _____

6. _____

7. _____

8. _____

9/10. Modern evolution scientists have been known to pick up a random rock and claiming it is an ape-man stone tool. List the location where two such examples were found.
LOCATION: _____
LOCATION: _____

This is the back side of a student handout page.

Answers Quiz A
Chapter 5
The Orce Ape-Man

1. skull (piece or fragment), and two arm bones (humerus) (page 175)
2. *Homo habilis* and *Homo erectus* (page 180)
3. Any 3 of the following: lemurs, monkeys, apes, humans, ape-men.
4. Donkey or ass
5. Internal crest (or bony crest, or crest)
6. Suture line (or wavy suture line or connection between two skull bones)
7. Any three of these answers (pages 184-185):
    - ape-man teenager (or 17 years old ape-man)
    - young ass (or donkey)
    - ape-man child (or 5 to 7 year old ape-man child)
    - zebra (or extinct zebra)
    - horse (or extinct horse)
    - ruminant

8-10. These three answers, any order:
   - Dr. Coppens --------Famous for leading the team that discovered Lucy
   - Dr. Howell--------Famous for creating a well-known human evolution chart (in *Early Man*)
   - Dr. Tobias--------Famous for naming and describing *Homo habilis*

Answers Quiz B
Chapter 5
The Orce Ape-Man

1. True (page 170 and 172)
2. True
3. True
4. False (one side was covered with sediment)
5. True
6. False (ruminant)
7. True
8. True
9. False (1,400)
10. True

Answers Quiz C
Chapter 5
The Orce Ape-Man

1. Over 300 (or 300) (page 180)

2. the lines where the skull bones attached to each other (page 182)

3. an *abnormally* wavy suture line and a large bony crest (page 182)

4. A

5-8. Any order
 -Piltdown Man (Chapter 4 page 91)

 -Nebraska Man (or pig tooth or *Hesperopithecus*) (Chapter 3 page 81)

 -*Tetraprothomo* (or Ameghino's ape-man in Argentina) (Chapter 2 page 19)

 -Orce Man (Chapter 5 page 190)

9/10. any order:
 -gravel in parking lot (Dr. Martucci)

 -rock outside bedroom (Dr. Mason)

CHAPTER 6

Teacher's Notes for Week 15
Teacher time for this class: 10 minutes

TEACHER STEP 1: Pass out Student Objectives Sheet for Chapter 6, The Libyan Ape-Man (pages that follow.) Tell students that during class today they should work filling out the Student Objectives Sheet. What they do not finish in class will be their homework.

TEACHER STEP 2 (END OF CLASS): Read Out loud: There will be a quiz at the beginning of class next week on the Student Objectives Sheet for Chapter 6, The Libyan Ape-Man which you are working on. If you study these sheets you should be able to get a 100%.

This is the back side of a teacher page.

CHAPTER 6

Student Objectives Sheet for Chapter 6 The Libyan Ape-Man (5 Pages)

By studying these objectives and knowing this core information, you should be able to pass the quiz at the beginning of class next week.

1. The student should be able to identify where Libya is (what continent and what part of continent) (page 207).

2. The student should name the three fossil bones (body parts) which made up the Libyan ape-man (page 207).

3. The student should know what scientist heavily influenced Dr. Boaz when he was a high school student. Specifically, what was the name of the scientist, the name of the book that the scientist wrote, and specifically which diagram in that book that heavily influenced Dr. Boaz (page 208)?

4. The student should know how many fossil expeditions Dr. Boaz directed in Africa (page 208).

5. The student should know what museum did Dr. Boaz founded (page 209).

6. The student should know what position did Dr. Boaz held at New York University (page 209 middle).

7. The student should know what discovery Dr. Boaz is known for among evolutionary scientists (page 210).

8. The student should know what the full formal name of Dr. Boaz's fossil expedition to Sahabi, Libya North Africa (page 210).

9. The student should know what organization funded Dr. Boaz's first full dig season in Libya (top page 211).

10. The student should be able to name FROM MEMORY the three ape-man fossils Dr. Boaz's team found and the year that each fossil was found (page 212).

11. The student should know what Dr. Boaz concluded he had found (in these three fossils) (page 212).

12. The student should know that the famous ape-man collarbone from Libya that Dr. Boaz identified was initially identified by Dr. Jean de Heinzelin as what kind of bone (page 214).

(Continued on next page)

113

CHAPTER 6

13. Dr. Boaz thought the primate collarbone found by Dr. de Heinzelin was not a mammal rib but a collarbone. He thought it was not an ordinary primate collarbone. What two features did the collarbone possess that made it unusual (page 214)?

14. The student should know what four types of animals make up the evolutionary term "hominoid" (page 260 appendix D).

15. When Dr. Boaz initially published his article about the collarbone he said it was a hominoid collarbone (page 215). The student should know what four types of animals this collarbone could belong to if it was a hominoid collarbone (see previous question and page 260 appendix D).

16. The student should know that Dr. Boaz, using a microscope, could see the attachment points of shoulder muscles (pectoralis, deltoid) on the collarbone (page 216).

17. The student should know that Dr. Boaz concluded that since the collarbone had the shape of both an ape and a human, it must be an ape-man collarbone (page 216).

18. The student should know the angle of the collarbone in these three animals (page 218):
    - Chimp
    - Human
    - The Libyan ape-man collarbone

19. The student should know that Dr. Boaz thought the Libyan collarbone was from an animal partway evolved between an ape and a human since the angle of the collarbone in the Libyan creature was between the collarbone angle of an ape and a human (page 218).

20. The student should know that Dr. Boaz thought that because the Libyan collarbone had a backward-S curve which is characteristic of humans and ape-men, it suggested this creature walked in what manner (biped or quadruped) (page 218).

21. The student should know how old that Dr. Boaz thought the Libyan ape-man was (in millions of years) (bottom page 218).

22. The student should know that Dr. Boaz thought his upright-walking ape-man from Libya was older than Lucy. Up until that point, Lucy was thought to be the oldest upright-walking, bipedal ape-man (page 218).

23. The student should know the names of the two bones in the lower leg: The tibia is the big bone of the lower leg and is located towards the inside. The fibula is the smaller bone of the lower leg and is the outside bone of the lower leg. The student should be able to feel and identify these two bones in their own leg.

(Continued on next page)

CHAPTER 6

24. The student should know if the lower leg bone found by Dr. Boaz was a tibia or fibula (page 219).

25. The student should know that Dr. Boaz determined the fossil fibula he found in Libya looked surprisingly like a _____ (kind of animal) and very unlike a _____ (kind of animal) (page 219).

26. The student should know that since Dr. Boaz suggested the fibula from Libya was attached to a human-like foot, what did this imply about how his ape-man walked (page 219)?

27. The student should know the location of the big toe in relation to the rest of the foot in apes and humans and be able to identify an ape or a human foot from seeing just the bones, such as these two pictures (page 219).

28. The student should know Dr. Boaz determined the brain size of the Libyan ape-man to be what size, based on the skull fragment (page 220).

29. The student should know what Dr. Boaz told an Associated Press reporter what about the age of Lucy (page 225).

30. The student should know that Dr. Boaz told an Associated Press reporter that since Lucy was younger than originally thought and was incorrectly dated, and this meant what (page 225).

31. The student should know that Dr. Boaz a reporter from *The New York Times* that the famous ape-man Lucy was misidentified by Dr. Johanson. The student should that Dr. Johanson identified Lucy as the species *Australopithecus afarensis* but Dr. Boaz thought Lucy was actually what species (page 225).

32. The student should know what unwritten rule among human evolution scientists that Dr. Boaz broke which made Dr. Johanson and his partner Dr. White so angry (page 225).

33. The student should be able to write out, FROM MEMORY, the three claims (underlined below) that Dr. Boaz made to reporters about the famous ape-man Lucy:
    -Lucy was misdated (and was younger than previously thought)
    -Lucy was misidentified (and was not a new species but was
        Australopithecus africanus)
    -Lucy was not a human ancestor (Lucy not important in human evolution)

34. When Dr. Johanson's partner Dr. White began to investigate Dr. Boaz's famous ape-man collarbone, he determined it was actually from what type of animal? (page 228). BE SPECIFIC
    Body part: "Posterior..._____"
    Animal: "Pacific..._____"

(Continued on next page)

CHAPTER 6

35. The student should know if the Libyan ape-man collarbone was from a dolphin, the collarbone was no longer from the mammal order Primates, but was from the mammal order Cetacea which includes whales and dolphins. IMPORTANT.

36. The student should be able to write out from memory the name of the mammal order which includes whales and dolphins.

37. The student should know what kind of animal Dr. Andrew Hill determined the Libyan ape-man skull was from (page 230).

38. The student should know that, in general, monkeys are much smaller than apes and have much smaller brains than apes.

39. The student should know that if the skull of the Libyan ape-man is actually a monkey as Dr. Andrew Hill suggested, then it could not have a "relatively large brain" as Dr. Boaz initially claimed.

40. The student should know what kind of animal Dr. Andrew Hill determined the Libyan ape-man fibula to be (page 230).

41. The student should know that if the fibula was not from a primate as Dr. Andrew Hill suggested, then this suggests it would not be attached to a human-like foot as Dr. Boaz initially claimed.

42. The student should know that the scientist working with Dr. Boaz, including experts in dolphins and whales (Dr. Daryl Domning, marine mammal specialist at Howard University), and experts in monkeys and apes (two anthropologists, two paleontologists) did not correct or contradict Dr. Boaz's ape-man fossil claim. It was only when Dr. Boaz crossed the red line and publicly humiliated Dr. Johanson's and White's ape-man called Lucy, did scientists begin to speak up.

43. In hindsight, Dr. Boaz identified a dolphin's rib as an ape-man that walked upright. How many incorrect anatomical features did Dr. Boaz see which indicated to him this dolphin rib was an ape-man collarbone (page 234).

44. The student should know the shape of what letter of the alphabet (A-Z) a mammal rib and a mammal collarbone have (page 236).

45. The student should know if a mammal rib and a mammal collarbone are simply turned over they will then have the shape of a backward-C shape or a backward-S shape, but even so, they are sill C-shaped and S-shaped (page 236).

(Continued on next page)

CHAPTER 6

46. The student should be able to identify a rib and a collarbone from their shape using photos such as these shown here (page 236).

47. The student should know that Dr. Boaz's "collarbone" with a "backward-S shape" was really a rib with a C-shape. Dr. Boaz simply imagined it had a S-shape (page 236).

48. The student should know why Boaz's logic was flawed when he said that a backward-S curve of a collarbone implies that the creature might be bipedal (walked on two feet like a human) (bottom page 236).

49. The student should know that Dr. Boaz was aware that dolphin bones had been found at the same dig site where his supposed "ape-man collarbone" was found (page 237).

50. The student should know that Dr. Boaz and Dr. Cramer violated the common sense rule named "Misidentifying Animals Found at Same Site as Ape-Man" (page 237). In retrospect, what should Dr. Boaz have done to avoid his disastrous mistake?

51. The student should know that the age for Dr. Boaz's fossil changed many times. Each time a different scientist came up with a different age (page 238).

52. Dr. Boaz's team found three fossils which they determined to be 1) an ape-man collarbone, 2) an ape-man fibula and 3) an ape-man skull. The student should know, specifically what did these three fossils turn out to be.

53. The student should know that the words clavicle and collarbone are synonymous and be able to point to and feel the collarbone with their fingertips on their own body.

(End Student Objectives Chapter 6)

This is the back side of a student handout page.

Teacher's Notes for Week 16
Teacher time for this class: 40 minutes

TEACHER STEP 1: Students take quiz. Pass out the "Chapter 6 Quiz, The Libyan Ape-Man" which are on the following pages. (You can choose from one of three sample quizzes, either Quiz A, B, C.) The quiz is only 10 questions long. Grade the quiz with the provided answer sheet (Either A, B, or C) and record the grade.

Next Chapter: Chapter 7 CONCLUSIONS

TEACHER STEP 2: After test corrected, lead class in class discussion.

Class Discussion Question #1. We are about to finish the book, what have you learned so far about the science of human evolution?

<u>Answer:</u> Let the students answer on own. Scientists can be wrong, can misidentify fossils etc.

Class Discussion Question #2. Has anyone in class read the next chapter, "*Chapter 7 Conclusions*"? If you have do not answer this next class discussion question so as to not spoil this for the other students.

The author has a surprise ending in Chapter 7. He left clues all along the way through the first 6 chapters. Here is a clue what the surprise is: What did all five ape-men in this book have in common—*Tetraprothomo* (Chapter 2), *Hesperopithecus* (Chapter 3), *Prometheus* (Chapter 4), Orce Man (Chapter 5), and the Libyan Hominid (Chapter 6)?

Answer: Let the students try to answer. Do not tell them the answer. When they have finished, tell them the answer is in the conclusions Chapter 7 which they are to read now in class (10 minutes). This chapter is only 2 pages long.

TEACHER STEP 3: Students should now read Chapter 7 in Class.

TEACHER STEP 4: Only *after* each student is finished reading Chapter 7, Conclusions, they may pick up the Student Objectives Sheet for Chapter 7 and begin to fill out.

TEACHER STEP 5: Read out loud at end of class: Next week there will be a quiz at the beginning of class on Chapter 7 Student Objectives Sheet.

This is the back side of a teacher page.

Name:_____   Date:_____

Chapter 6
The Libyan Hominid
Quiz A

Answer the following:

1. Write out the three ape-man fossils Dr. Boaz's team found. _____
   _____   _____

2. Dr. Boaz thought the "mammal rib" found by Dr. de Heinzelin was an unusual primate collarbone. What two features did the collarbone possess that made it unusual?
   _____   _____

3. Dr. Boaz thought the Libyan ape-man collarbone was intermediate in angle between an ape and a human collarbone. Of these three animals—a chimp, the Libyan ape-man collarbone, and a human—which collarbone angles upward most? _____

4. What kind of animal foot is this (right)?
   _____

5. What unwritten rule did Dr. Boaz break that ultimately caused his own ape-man to be overturned? _____

6. When Dr. Johanson's partner Dr. White began to investigate Dr. Boaz's famous ape-man collarbone, he determined it was actually from what type of animal?_____

7. When Dr. Johanson's partner Dr. White began to investigate Dr. Boaz's famous ape-man collarbone what <u>specific body part</u> did he determine it was actually from? _____

8. The Libyan ape-man collarbone was not even from a Primate. What <u>mammal order</u> did it turn out to be? _____

9. What kind of animal did Dr. Andrew Hill determine the Libyan ape-man <u>skull</u> to actually be?
   _____

10. What body part is this bone (right)? _____

121

This is the back side of a student handout page.

Name:_____   Date:_____

Chapter 6
The Libyan Hominid
Quiz B

True or False:

1. Libya is in Europe. _____

2. The three fossil bones that made up Dr. Boaz's ape-man were: a collarbone, a tibia, and a skull. _____

3. The four types of animals make up the evolutionary term "hominoid" are ape-men, humans, apes, and monkeys._____

4. Dr. Boaz concluded that since the collarbone had the shape of both an ape and a human, it must be an ape-man collarbone _____

5. Dr. Boaz determined the brain size of the Libyan ape-man to be small based on the skull fragment size. _____

6. Dolphins and fish are members of (the mammal order) Cetacea. _____

7. Dr. Boaz detected 4 anatomical features indicating a dolphin rib was an ape-man collarbone. _____

8. A mammal rib has the same shape as the letter L (page 236). _____

9. A primate collarbone has the shape as the letter C (page 236). _____

10. In retrospect, if Dr. Boaz had compared his supposed ape-man collarbone to the animals that had been found at the same dig site in Libya, he would have avoided a disastrous mistake. _____

This is the back side of a student handout page.

Name:_____   Date:_____

Chapter 6
The Libyan Hominid
Quiz C

Answer the following:

1. The famous fossil from Libya that Dr. Boaz identified as an ape-man collarbone was initially identified by Dr. Jean de Heinzelin as what kind of bone? _____

2. How old did Dr. Boaz think the Libyan ape-man was in years? _____

3. Dr. Boaz's team found three fossils which they determined to be an ape-man collarbone, an ape-man fibula, and an ape-man skull. In reality what did these three fossils turn out to be?
_____   _____   _____

4. What kind of animal foot is this?
_____

5. What unwritten rule did Dr. Boaz break that ultimately caused his own ape-man to be overturned? _____
_____

6. When Dr. Johanson's partner Dr. White began to investigate Dr. Boaz's famous ape-man collarbone, he determined it was actually from what type of animal?_____

7. When Dr. Johanson's partner Dr. White began to investigate Dr. Boaz's famous ape-man collarbone, what specific <u>body part</u> did he determine it was actually from (page 228)?
_____

8. The Libyan ape-man collarbone was not from a primate. What mammal <u>order</u> did it turn out to be? _____

9. What body part is this bone (RIGHT)?

10. Dr. Boaz said his ape-man collarbone had a "backward-S shape." In reality what shape was it? _____

125

This is the back side of a student handout page.

Answers Quiz A
Chapter 6
The Libyan Hominid

1. Any order: collarbone (or clavicle),

    skull bone

    fibula (or lower leg bone)

2. chimpanzee and human features (page 214)

3. chimp (page 218)

4. human (the big toe is next to the other toes)

5. bringing his disagreement with Johanson to the press (page 225)

6. dolphin or Pacific white-sided dolphin or *Lagenorhynchus obliquidens* (page 228).

7. rib or 7th rib or posterior 7th rib (page 228)

8. Cetacea or cetacean

9. monkey or monkey skull (page 230)

10. collarbone or clavicle (it is S-shaped)

Answers Quiz B
Chapter 6
The Libyan Hominid

1. False (North Africa)

2. False (collarbone, a fibula, and a skull)

3. False (ape-men, humans, apes, and extinct apes (page 260)

4. True (page 216)

5. False (large-brained) (page 220)

6. False (dolphins and whales. Dosphins are mammals. Fish are not mammals)

7. False (18) (page 234)

8. False (the letter C)

9. False (the letter S)

10. True (see Lesson Concerning Misidentifying Animals Found at Same Site as Ape-Man page 237)

ANSWER SHEETS

Answers Quiz C
Chapter 6
The Libyan Hominid

1. mammal rib

2. 5 million years old (bottom page 218)

3. a dolphin rib, a monkey skull, and a non-primate fibula

4. an ape (the big toe is spread out from the other toes)

5. a scientist should not bring a disagreement with another scientist over an ape-man fossil to the press (page 225)

6. a dolphin or Pacific white-sided dolphin or *Lagenorhynchus obliquidens* (page 228)

7. rib or 7th rib or posterior 7th rib (page 228)

8. Cetacea or cetacean

9. rib (it is C-shaped)

10. C-shaped

CHAPTER 7

Student Objectives Sheet for Chapter 7 Conclusions (2 pages)

By studying these objectives and knowing this core information, you should be able to pass the quiz at the beginning of class next week.

1. The student should know what the five ape-men covered in this book have in common—*Tetraprothomo* (Chapter 2), *Hesperopithecus* (Chapter 3), *Prometheus* (Chapter 4), Orce Man (Chapter 5), and the Libyan Hominid (Chapter 6).

2. The student should be able to fill in <u>the non-primate animal bone</u>(s) or <u>teeth</u> that were used to create these five ape-men:
    Chapter 2 *Tetraprothomo*
        Leg bone _____ (page 21)
    Chapter 3 Nebraska Ape-Man, *Hesperopithecus*
        Tooth _____ (page 79)
    Chapter 4 *Australopithecus prometheus*
        Upper ape-man arm bone fossil MLD 15 _____ (page 154-155)
        Ape-man skull bones fossils MLD 26, 33 _____ (page 154-155)
        Ape-man collarbones fossils MLD 20, 36 _____ (page 154-155)
        Ape-man hip bone fossil MLD 17 _____ (page 154-155)
    Chapter 5 Orce Ape-Man
        Orce ape-man skull fossil VM-0 _____ (page 182)
        Orce ape-man tooth fossil BL5-0 _____ (bottom page 189)
        Orce ape-man humerus VM-1960 _____ (page 186 bottom)
    Chapter 6 Libyan Ape-Man
        Libyan ape-man collarbone _____ (page 229)
        Libyan ape-man fibula _____ (page 230)

3. The student should know how many professional evolution scientists promoted these five ape-men (listed above) which were created from non-primate mammal bones (page 241).

4. The student should know <u>how many evolution books</u> were written by professional scientists who promoted these five ape-men which were created from non-primate mammal bones (page 241).

5. The student should know <u>how many museums</u> were <u>directed</u> by professional scientists who promoted these five ape-men which were created from non-primate mammal bones (page 241).

6. The student should know <u>how many museums</u> were <u>founded</u> by professional scientists who promoted these five ape-men which were created from non-primate mammal bones (page 241).

(Continued on next page)

Chapter 7

7. The student should know <u>how many random rocks</u> these scientists interpreted to be ape-man "stone tools" but later turned out to be from ape-men created from non-primate mammal bones (page 241).

8. The student should know <u>how many random animal bones</u> were interpreted to be ape-man "bone tools" but later turned out to be from ape-men created from non-primate mammal bones (page 241).

9. The student should know the total number of ape-men species which were promoted in the past, which have subsequently been overturned.

10. The student should be able to write out, FROM MEMORY, the 9 categories of overturned ape-men used by the author. IMPORTANT

    Ape-Men Created From Non-Primate Mammal Bones (this book)

    Ape-Men Created Using Reptile Bones (next book in this series);

    Ape-Men Created Using Monkey Bones (next book in this series);

    Ape-Men Created Using Ape Bones (next book in this series);

    Ape-Men Created by Scientists Altering Fossils (next book in this series);

    Ape-Men Created From Living Human Beings (next book in this series);

    Ape-Men Created From Recently Buried Human Beings (next book in this series);

    Ape-Men Created From Humans Buried More Than 2,000 Years Ago (next book in this series);

    Ape-Men Created From Robust Australopithecines (next book in this series).

(End of Student Objectives Sheet
Chapter 7 Conclusions)

Teacher's Notes for Week 17
Teacher time for this class: 20 minutes

TEACHER STEP 1: Students take quiz. Pass out the "Chapter 7 Conclusion" quiz which are on the following pages. (You can choose from one of three sample quizzes, either Quiz A, B, C.) The quiz is only 10 questions long. Grade the quiz with the provided answer sheet (Either A, B, or C) and record the grade.

TEACHER STEP 2: Read out loud. Next week is the comprehensive final exam. It will have 20 questions and will be worth 20% of your semester grade for this course. To prepare for the exam, you should study the all of the Student Objective Sheets which you have already filled out, for Chapters 1-7.

TEACHER STEP 3: During the rest of the class you should study for the final exam. Remember, all of the 20 questions will come off the Student Objective Sheets. If anyone wants to watch the DVD on their own they can do that anytime they wish after class.

This is the back side of a teacher page.

Chapter 7
Conclusions
Quiz A

1. How many species of ape-men, promoted in the past, have subsequently been overturned?

2-9. Write out the nine categories of overturned ape-men (any order):

2. _____

3. _____

4. _____

5. _____

6. _____

7. _____

8. _____

9. _____

10. _____

This is the back side of a student handout page.

Chapter 7
Conclusions
Quiz B

True or False:

1. Professional scientists who promoted ape-men created from non-primate mammal bones directed more than 100 museums. _____

2. More than 3,000 random animal bones were interpreted to be "ape-man bone tools" used by ape-men created from non-primate mammal bones (page 241). _____

3. More than 16,000 random rocks were interpreted to be "ape-man stone tools" used by ape-men created from non-primate mammal bones (page 241). _____

4. The leg bone of *Tetraprothomo* was from a antelope. _____

5. The Orce ape-man tooth was from a hippopotamus. _____

6. The Libyan ape-man collarbone was from a cat. _____

7. The two collarbones of *Australopithecus prometheus* were horse toe bones. _____

8. The hip bone of *Australopithecus prometheus* was a cat hip bone. _____

9. The Nebraska ape-man tooth was actually a hippo tooth. _____

10. Two skull bones of *Australopithecus prometheus* were bovid bones. _____

This is the back side of a student handout page.

Chapter 7
Conclusions
Quiz C

1. What did the five ape-men covered in this book (*Tetraprothomo,* Nebraska Ape-Man, *Australopithecus prometheus,* Orce ape-man, Libyan ape-man) have in common?

_____

2. How many professional evolution scientists promoted ape-men which were created from non-primate mammal bones? _____

3. How many evolution books were written by these professional scientists who promoted ape-men created from non-primate mammal bones? _____

4-10. Fill in the non-primate animal that were used to create these ape-men:

4. *Tetraprothomo* leg bone _____

5. Nebraska Ape-Man tooth _____

6. *Australopithecus prometheus* upper arm bone MLD 15 _____

7. *Australopithecus prometheus* collarbones MLD 20, 36 (BE CAREFUL, THIS IS NOT THE LIBYAN APE-MAN COLLARBONE) _____

8. Orce ape-man skull _____

9. Orce ape-man tooth BL5-0 _____

10. Libyan ape-man collarbone _____

This is the back side of a student handout page.

Answers Quiz A
Chapter 7
Conclusions

1. 200 or more than 200 (page 241)

2-10. Any order:

   Ape-Men Created From Non-primate Mammal Bones

   Ape-Men Created Using Reptile Bones;

   Ape-Men Created Using Monkey Bones;

   Ape-Men Created Using Ape Bones;

   Ape-Men Created by Scientists Altering Fossils;

   Ape-Men Created From Living Human Beings,

   Ape-Men Created From Recently Buried Human Beings;

   Ape-Men Created From Humans Buried More Than 2,000 Years Ago,

   Ape-Men Created From Robust Australopithecines

Answers Quiz B
Chapter 7
Conclusions

1. False

2. True (3200)

3. True

4. False (procyonid or raccoon family)

5. True

6. False (dolphin or cetacean)

7. True

8. True

9. False (pig tooth)

10. True

Answers Quiz C
Chapter 7
Conclusions

1. They all contained bones of non-primate mammals.

2. 40

3. 128 (or more than 100 or any number above 100)

4. procyonid (or raccoon family)

5. pig (or *Prosthennops* or artiodactyl)

6. canid (or dog family)

7. horse toe bones (or horse or equid)

8. donkey (or ass or equid or zebra or horse)

9. hippo or hippopotamus

10. dolphin (or Pacific white-sided dolphin or Cetacea or cetacean or whale family)

Teacher's Notes for Week 18
Teacher time for this class: 30-70 minutes

TEACHER STEP 1: Students take the Final Comprehensive Exam. Pass out the exam which are on the following pages. (You can choose from one of three sample final exams, either A, B, C.) The test is only 20 questions long. Grade the quiz with the provided answer sheet (Either A, B, or C) and record the grade.

PLEASE NOTE. THE FINAL EXAMS HAVE EXTRA CREDIT QUESTIONS SO IT IS POSSIBLE TO GET MORE THAN 20 ANSWERS CORRECT. WHEN YOU RECORD THE SCORES FOR THE FINAL EXAM, RECORD THE TOTAL NUMBER OF CORRECT ANSWERS.

TEACHER STEP 2: (OPTIONAL). Play the entire DVD, *Untold Stories of Human Evolution*.

TEACHER STEP 3: (OPTIONAL). Build excitement for next semester by discussing the follow-up course (*Volume 4, Evolution: The Grand Experiment, Nine Categories of Overturned Ape-Men*). You can tell the students that next semester they will learn about the other 200 species of ape-men that have been disproved and also about widespread fraud which has been uncovered involving ape-men.

This is the back side of a teacher page.

Comprehensive Final Exam A

1. How many different species of ape-men did Florentino Ameghino create using bones dug up from the graves of recently buried humans?

2. How many animals in the human evolution chart shown below turned out to be just ordinary apes or just ordinary *Homo sapien*s? _____

3. What did Dr. Ameghino think the scoriae found at Mount Hermoso represented? _____

4. *True or False*: Humans and apes are habitual bipeds. _____

5. *True or False*: The Libyan ape-man collarbone was from a cat. _____

6. How many ape-men, promoted in the past, have subsequently been overturned? _____

7. What did the *Australopithecus prometheus* collarbones MLD 20, 36 turn out to be? (BE CAREFUL, THIS IS NOT THE LIBYAN APE-MAN COLLARBONE) _____

8. What is the formal species names that Dr. Dart initially assigned to his first ape-man discovered in 1924 and to his second ape-man discovered in 1947?
    1924: _____
    1947: _____

9. The first skull of *Australopithecus prometheus* that Dr. Dart submitted to *Nature* but which he had to quickly retract turned out to be the skull of what kind of animal? _____

10. What are the three types of great apes living today? _____
 _____ _____

11. Dr. Charles K. (Bob) Brain demonstrated that Dr. Dart's australopithecine bones did not get to the caves because they lived in the cave but they were brought to the cave by _____.

12. What animal did the leg bone of the ape-man *Tetraprothomo* turn out to be? _____

(Continued on next page)

143

13-15. Matching. Place the letter A or B next to each pelvis

13. Human pelvis _____

14. Ape pelvis _____

15. *Australopithecus* pelvis_____

A. Upper pelvis turns forward 90 degrees

B. Upper pelvis goes out sideways

16. Three ape-man fossils were found near Orce, Spain at the Venta Micena dig site. What body parts were these? _____   _____   _____

17. Dr. Boaz thought the Libyan ape-man collarbone was intermediate in angle between an ape and a human collarbone. Of these three animals—an ape, the Libyan ape-man collarbone, and a human—which collarbone angles upward most? _____

18.. What kind of animal foot is this (right)?_____

19. What did the five ape-men covered in this book (*Tetraprothomo,* Nebraska Ape-Man, *Australopithecus prometheus,* Orce ape-man, Libyan ape-man) have in common?

_____

20. How many professional evolution scientists promoted ape-men which were created from non-primate mammal bones? _____

EXTRA CREDIT

21. Write out Dr. Dart's 12 word quote which indicated he was willing to make up stories about ape-men. "Never _____
_____ "

22. Write out from memory the subtitle of the speech that Dr. Osborn gave at the American Philosophical Society. (6 or 7 words total) "Let us _____
_____

23. Write out the *The New York Times* statement which said the Nebraska ape-man tooth had been investigated thoroughly by evolution scientists. (Approximately 25 words.)
_____
_____
_____

THE FINAL EXAMS HAVE EXTRA CREDIT QUESTIONS SO IT IS POSSIBLE TO GET MORE THAN 20 ANSWERS CORRECT. WHEN YOU RECORD THE SCORES FOR THE FINAL EXAM, RECORD THE TOTAL NUMBER OF CORRECT ANSWERS.

(END)

Comprehensive Final Exam B

1. *True or False*: The latest, most up to date fossil evidence offered for human evolution (*Homo naledi, Sahelanthropus tchadensis, Australopithecus sediba*) is not controversial among evolution scientists. _____

2. What was so ironic about Dr. Ameghino's mistaken identification of the ape-man leg bone found at Mount Hermoso? _____
_____

3. *True or False*: Dr. Florentino Ameghino was considered by his colleagues as one of the most eminent geologists and paleontologists of his day. _____

4. The famous Nebraska Ape-Man tooth was actually what? _____

5. *True or False*: A skull of a modern baby chimpanzee looks like the skull of an adult chimpanzee. _____

6. The reliability of any fossil interpretation is proportional to what determination?
_____

7. Dart's reconstructed pelvis of *Australopithecus prometheus* looked nearly identical to the pelvis of what animal? _____

8. What was the name of the Hollywood movie that was based on Dr. Dart's tool-using, fire-using, head-bashing, large-brained ape-man? _____

9. Name the three ape-men endorsed by Dr. Grafton Elliot Smith which turned out to be NOT ape-men. _____ _____
_____

10. The ODK bone tool culture is an acronym for "ape-man bone tools" found at Makapansgat. Write out the full name for ODK. _____

11. *True or False*: 2400 stone tools were found by Dr. Dart's team at Makapansgat and all turned out to be just rocks. _____

12. *True or False*: The Taung Child, Prometheus, and Mrs. Ples turned out to be the same species. _____

13. What are the three types great apes living today? _____ _____
_____

14. Dr. Charles K. (Bob) Brain demonstrated that Dr. Dart's australopithecine bones did not get to the caves because they lived in the cave but they were brought to the cave by _____.

(Continued on next page)

145

15. *True or False:* The Orce ape-man tooth was from a hippopotamus. _____

16-18. Matching. Place the letter A or B next to each pelvis

16. Human pelvis _____   A. Upper pelvis turns forward 90 degrees

17. Ape pelvis _____   B. Upper pelvis goes out sideways

18. *Australopithecus* pelvis_____

19. Scientists described the Orce ape-man skull to reporters at the press conference in 1983 as an ape-man partway evolved between what two other ape-men? _____ _____

20. *True or False*: The leg bone of *Tetraprothomo* was from a antelope. _____

EXTRA CREDIT

21. Write out Dr. Dart's 12 word quote which indicated he was willing to make up stories about ape-men. "Never _____ _____ "

22. Write out from memory the subtitle of the speech that Dr. Osborn gave at the American Philosophical Society. (6 or 7 words total) "Let us _____ _____

23. Write out the *The New York Times* statement which said the Nebraska ape-man tooth had been investigated thoroughly. (Approximately 25 words.)
_____
_____
_____

THE FINAL EXAMS HAVE EXTRA CREDIT QUESTIONS SO IT IS POSSIBLE TO GET MORE THAN 20 ANSWERS CORRECT. WHEN YOU RECORD THE SCORES FOR THE FINAL EXAM, RECORD THE TOTAL NUMBER OF CORRECT ANSWERS.

(END)

Comprehensive Final Exam C

1. *True or False*: *Initially* scientists thought the fossil *Oreopithecus* was an ape-man. _____

2. What did Dr. Ameghino's ape-man "scoriae" turned out to be? _____

3. What did Dr. Aleš Hrdlička conclude about Dr. Ameghino's five ape men which appeared in his human evolution charts? _____

4. What was so ironic about Dr. Osborn criticizing William Jennings Bryan for not agreeing that the fossil tooth found in Nebraska was an ape-man? _____
_____

5. Name ONE of the three high profile scientists that endorsed the Orce man and what they were famous for: _____ _____

6. *True or False*: When Dr. Dart initially announced many discoveries about the controlled use of fire and bone tools used by the ape-man *Australopithecus prometheus*, there seemed little reason to doubt the authenticity of Dart's fire-using, bone-tool using ape-man._____

7. Dart told *The New York Times* the brain size of australopithecines were how large (in cc) and equivalent in size to what animal brain? _____ cc _____.

8. What are the three types great apes living today? _____ _____
_____

9. Dr. Charles K. (Bob) Brain demonstrated that Dr. Dart's australopithecine bones did not get to the caves because they lived in the cave but they were brought to the cave by _____.

10. *True or False*: The Orce ape-man skull was initially thought to be the oldest ape-man ever to be discovered in Europe and Asia. _____

11-13. Matching. Place the letter A or B next to each pelvis

11. Human pelvis _____   A. Upper pelvis turns forward 90 degrees

12. Ape pelvis _____   B. Upper pelvis goes out sideways

13. *Australopithecus* pelvis_____

14. When Dr. Johanson's partner Dr. White began to investigate Dr. Boaz's famous ape-man collarbone, he determined it was actually from what type of animal? _____

15. *True or False*: Lemurs, monkeys, and apes belong to the mammal order Primates. _____

16. *True or False*: Even after the 1984 revelation that the Orce ape-man skull was from a baby ass, scientists continue to promote the skull as an ape-man. _____

(Continued on next page)

17. When Dr. Marie de Lumley saw the inside of the Orce skull fully exposed for the first time, she saw features A and B (below) and said it was what kind of animal? _____

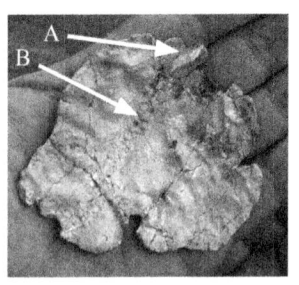

18. Dr. Gibert was accused of fraud for supplying a fraudulent drawing of the Orce man suture line. Which of these drawings did he supply, A or B (below)? _____

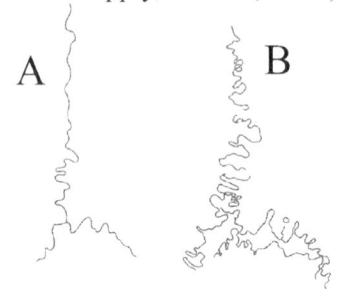

19. What body part is this bone (right)? _____

20. *True or False*: Evolution scientists first thought the bone found in Orce was an ape-man humerus. Now Dr. Bienvenido Martínez believes it is an elephant leg bone. _____

EXTRA CREDIT

21. Write out Dr. Dart's 12 word quote which indicated he was willing to make up stories about ape-men. "Never _____"

22. Write out from memory the subtitle of the speech that Dr. Osborn gave at the American Philosophical Society. (6 or 7 words total) "Let us _____
_____

23. Write out the *The New York Times* statement which said the Nebraska ape-man tooth had been investigated thoroughly. (Approximately 25 words.)
_____
_____
_____

THE FINAL EXAMS HAVE 3 EXTRA CREDIT QUESTIONS SO IT IS POSSIBLE TO GET MORE THAN 20 ANSWERS CORRECT. WHEN YOU RECORD THE SCORES FOR THE FINAL EXAM, RECORD THE TOTAL NUMBER OF CORRECT ANSWERS.

(END)

Answers
Comprehensive Final Exam A

1. 5

2. all or 5

3. fireplace or controlled use of fire

4. false (apes are quadrupeds)

5. false (dolphin rib)

6. 230 (or more than 200 or any number above 200)

7. horse toe bones

8. 1924: *Australopithecus africanus*

    1947: *Australopithecus prometheus*

9. baboon

10. gorilla, chimpanzee and orangutan (any order)

11. leopards (or animals or hyena or bird or eagle or porcupine)

12. procyonid (or raccoon or raccoon family or carnivore)

13. A

14. B

15. B

16. skull and two upper arm bones (or skull and two humerus or skull and lower leg bone of ruminant or antelope)

17. ape (or chimp)

18. human

19. all five had bones (and/or teeth) of non-primate mammals

20. 40

EXTRA CREDIT

21. "Never let the truth get in the way of a good story"

22. "Let Us Abandon the Ape-Human Theory"

23. "In the whole history of anthropology no tooth has ever been subjected to such severe cross-examination as this now world-famous tooth of *Hesperopithecus*."

THE FINAL EXAMS HAVE 3 EXTRA CREDIT QUESTIONS SO IT IS POSSIBLE TO GET MORE THAN 20 ANSWERS CORRECT. WHEN YOU RECORD THE SCORES FOR THE FINAL EXAM, RECORD THE TOTAL NUMBER OF CORRECT ANSWERS.

Answers
Comprehensive Final Exam B

1. false

2. He was an expert in procyonids (raccoon family) yet he identified a procyonid (raccoon family) leg bone as an ape-man leg bone.

3. true

4. pig (or *Prosthennops*)

5. false

6. The completeness of the skeleton

7. human

8. *2001: A Space Odyssey*

9. Neanderthal Man, Nebraska Man, Piltdown Man

10. Osteodontokeratic

11. false

12. true

13. gorilla, chimpanzee and orangutan

14. leopards (or hyenas or porcupines or birds or eagles or animals)

15. true

16. A

17. B

18. B

19. *Homo habilis* and *Homo erectus* (either order)

20. false

EXTRA CREDIT

21. "Never let the truth get in the way of a good story"

22. "Let Us Abandon the Ape-Human Theory"

23. "In the whole history of anthropology no tooth has ever been subjected to such severe cross-examination as this now world-famous tooth of *Hesperopithecus*."

THE FINAL EXAMS HAVE 3 EXTRA CREDIT QUESTIONS SO IT IS POSSIBLE TO GET MORE THAN 20 ANSWERS CORRECT. WHEN YOU RECORD THE SCORES FOR THE FINAL EXAM, RECORD THE TOTAL NUMBER OF CORRECT ANSWERS.

Answers
Comprehensive Final Exam C

1. true

2. pumice or lava rock

3. all had bones from recently buried human beings

4. it turned out to be a pig

5. Any one of these three answers:

    -Dr. Coppens --------Famous for leading the team that discovered Lucy

    -Dr. Howell--------Famous for creating a well-known human evolution chart (in *Early Man*)

    -Dr. Tobias--------Famous for naming and describing *Homo habilis*

6. true

7. 1000 cc   human

8. gorilla, chimpanzee, orangutan

9. leopards (or hyenas or birds or eagles or porcupines or animals)

10. true

11. A

12. B

13. B

14. dolphin or Pacific white-sided dolphin or *Lagenorhynchus obliquidens* (page 228)

15. true

16. true

17. donkey or ass

18. A

19. collarbone or clavicle

20. false

EXTRA CREDIT

21. "Never let the truth get in the way of a good story"

22. "Let Us Abandon the Ape-Human Theory"

23. "In the whole history of anthropology no tooth has ever been subjected to such severe cross-examination as this now world-famous tooth of *Hesperopithecus*."

THE FINAL EXAMS HAVE 3 EXTRA CREDIT QUESTIONS SO IT IS POSSIBLE TO GET MORE THAN 20 ANSWERS CORRECT. WHEN YOU RECORD THE SCORES FOR THE FINAL EXAM, RECORD THE TOTAL NUMBER OF CORRECT ANSWERS.

Printed in Great Britain
by Amazon